Is your God too small?

The Bible Reading Fellowship
15 The Chambers, Vineyard
Abingdon OX14 3FE
brf.org.uk

The Bible Reading Fellowship (BRF) is a Registered Charity (233280)

ISBN 978 0 85746 633 4
First published 2018
10 9 8 7 6 5 4 3 2 1 0
All rights reserved

Acknowledgements

A catalogue record for this book is available from the British Library

Printed and bound by CPI Group (UK) Ltd, Croydon CR0 4YY

Is your God too small?

David C. Potter

To Madeleine

We have walked a long way together.
With you and through you I have learnt so much of grace and love,
of faith and perseverance,
and of beauty.

Foreword

It was a kind gift to a young student of theology: *Your God Is Too Small* by J.B. Phillips, published in 1957. Somehow, I never got around to reading it. The book remained on my shelves for decades, still unread, until at some stage it was lent or lost, given or sold. Yet there are few books that have had a more long-term influence on my spiritual and theological development. The title remained with me as a constant challenge to my faith, doubts and fears. 'Your God is too small' was the phrase that came to mind when, after years of evasion, I finally got around to studying the book of Job.

'Have you considered my servant Job?' was God's question to Satan. It could well be God's challenge to us too. Some books of the Bible seem just too obscure, too long and too demanding for the pace of life in the 21st century. The book of Job is one of them. It is a story so different that we ignore it rather than struggle with its rhetoric. For years, that was what I had done and only now do I realise how much I have been missing that could have helped me through the unavoidable struggles and challenges of living as a Christian in the modern era.

For some years, I have found the IVP series, 'The Bible Speaks Today', very helpful in my daily Bible readings. Using *The Message of Job* by David Atkinson from the series, I steadily worked my way through the book with a growing sense of excitement and wonder. When I reached the end, I started again, this time also using the Tyndale Commentary on Job by Francis Andersen and referring occasionally to other, but less helpful, commentaries I have.

How to use this book

The place to start is with the book of Job itself. Take time to read it through. Use a modern translation; the New International Version is as good as you will find. This will give you a feel for the book. Don't worry at this stage if you find it hard to follow. It will also be helpful to read the relevant Bible passage as you come to the section which considers it.

Next, read the Introduction which follows (starting on p. 9). It provides some background to the book of Job. The meat of this book is divided into sections following the content of Job. You will find that each section covers a number of chapters of Job, which are introduced to help you understand their content better. You will find some issues are dealt with separately by way of additional information, some are developed in a more devotional style and, at the end of each section, there are questions to help you 'earth' what you have read. Why not open a journal and write your response to these questions?

Be sure to ask for the help of the Holy Spirit as you read. After all, he inspired the writer of the book of Job so is well placed to inspire you through it!

Contents

Part III: It's beyond me (chapters 38—42:6)

Introduction

Why? It was probably the first question we ever asked and we may well be asking it still as our lives come to an end. The young child is overwhelmed with discovery and demands urgent explanations for the world that fills its small horizons. The car starts – why? The sun, as we say, 'goes in' – why? Steam rises from the kettle spout – why? On and on, the questions are endless. Or it comes in response to a command: 'Don't step into the road!' – why? 'Don't run!' – why? Or, a few years later but with a different tone of voice, 'Don't stay out late tonight!' – why not? 'Don't answer back!' – why not?

But when we reach adulthood, the question assumes a darker shading. We want answers to bigger mysteries that stalk the path of every thinking person, and the greatest mystery seems to be human suffering. We need to understand. We pound the door of heaven for explanations which will address the seeming injustices of pain and tragedy, each bitter tear a question mark. Many give this as their reason for refusing to believe in God. It is not that their atheism is so strong but that their 'faith' is so weak.

We believe we can find the answers to these dilemmas with our technology and scientific knowledge. Surely, in our day more than any before, such basic questions must yield their mysteries. What really did happen on Bloody Sunday? Why did 96 football supporters die that day at Hillsborough? What really was said and done by whom, and when, in the debacle we call 'the Iraq war'? These are but a few of the enquiries lasting years and costing millions where every crumb of evidence was examined to answer the same haunting question: why? And when the millions of words are read, the tears shed, the fingers pointed, the experts have spoken and the reports are gathering dust on the shelf, we discover that they have addressed the wrong question. All they can tell us is the 'how?' or the 'who?' or the 'what?', but not the 'why?'.

When the serpent tempted Eve with the promise, 'You will be as gods,' he offered the possibility of an explanation of all things, but he lied. We still look for the same power: the wisdom to understand – ourselves, our world, our God and his ways. We want to know.

The poem of Job reflects this struggle to understand God's way in the world and to find our place in the greater scheme of things. And it does so at the point where the struggle is most intense: in the place of suffering. As Job eventually emerges from the struggle once more to flourish, he still hasn't found 'the answer', nor has the reader, but both are given a new way of responding to God.

> The book does not set out to answer the problem of suffering, but to proclaim a God so great that no answer is needed.
> H.L. Ellison[1]

> We may regard it as one of the most original works in the poetry of mankind.
> R.H. Pfeiffer[2]

Those who have written more fully on the book of Job express astonishment at the wide range of issues to which it makes reference, the breadth of human experience from despair to moral outrage to the loneliness of one who feels abandoned by God. Its poetic beauty is unrivalled and at times stunning.

Job's is not a fast-moving story, told in short chapters with neat sound bites. The book moves forward slowly, argumentatively and, at times, mysteriously towards its climax. If, however, we can grasp its message, we will have a much more profound understanding of how God works in the world and of a wisdom that is infinitely superior to our own.

The book of Job fascinates scholars because it keeps so many secrets:

1 Who was Job? We want to know more about this man but, no matter how much we prise up the edges and corners of his story, we fall back on little more than guesswork. Job is almost unmentioned in the rest of the Bible or contemporary literature, even though his patience has become a proverb in itself. Although there is no external historical reference to Job the man, we can feel, as we read, that this is a real-life story we are reading. For anyone who has known deep suffering, Job's raw pain, his utter bewilderment, will have the ring of truth.

   It might be easier to answer questions of Job's identity if we could place him on the timeline of Old Testament history, but there are no references to contemporary events we can date. The fact that Job acts as a priest for his family suggests that he lived before Moses and the introduction of the Levitical priesthood, while linguistic clues place him closer to the exile, hundreds of years later.

2 Who wrote Job? We don't know; nor do we know how the book came to be written, and to be written in such a developed literary style. Clearly it wasn't Job; never once does he speak as the storyteller.

3 How is Job written? It is largely written as poetry, and Hebrew poetry at that. (See below for a brief explanation of Hebrew poetry.) Don't look for rhyming couplets! The poetry is very carefully constructed according to the literary norms of biblical poetry where 'rhythm' is in the repetition of ideas rather than sounds. This slows the pace of the discussion and may lend a slightly unreal quality to the exchanges.

   Translating the book of Job presents a challenge to scholars because so much of the language is obscure. It uses over 100 words otherwise unknown in any of the languages of the ancient Near East. So, if you find variation between versions of the book, do not be surprised; sometimes the translators have to make their best guess.

All such discussions are external to the book itself. The book of Job is unique, both within the Bible and also among the literature of the ancient Near East.[3] It 'is an astonishing mixture of almost every kind of literature to be found in the Old Testament. Many individual pieces can be isolated and identified as proverbs, riddles, hymns, laments, curses, lyrical nature poems.'[4] In its story and its telling, the voice of God will be heard, the chasm between human and divine wisdom will be seen, the limitations of our own perception will be drawn and the awe-inspiring wonder of God's grace in human experience will be revealed to a greater degree.

The outline of the book follows a form which shows great care on the part of the author. Our approach follows a simpler framework:

- Chapters 1—2: Prose prologue which sets the context of what follows
- Chapter 3—27: The discussion between Job and his friends
- Chapter 28: An interlude on wisdom
- Three monologues:
  - Chapters 29—31 by Job
  - Chapters 32—37 by Elihu
  - Chapters 38—41 by God
- Chapter 42: Job restored

Another way of reading Job is to see it as basically three approaches to suffering (with a prologue, an interlude and an epilogue):

- Looking back (3—27)
- Looking forward (29—37)
- Looking up (38—41)

Still another approach, using the same divisions (with a prologue, an interlude and an epilogue):

- Focus on suffering: its cause
- Focus on the sufferer: the purpose
- Focus on sovereignty: the solution

The book of Job is a rich mine which yields treasure found in few other places in scripture.

Wisdom literature

The book of Job is classed as belonging to the 'wisdom literature' of the Bible.

Every age had its 'wise men' who reflected upon their life and times. In the ancient Near East, notably in Egypt and Mesopotamia, rulers gained prestige and political power as much for their wisdom as for their military might. A professional class developed to serve this need, men whose role was to reflect on the meaning and purpose of existence, the deeper issues of humanity's relationship to God. They became a sort of 'think tank' for the pharaohs and kings of the ancient world, the 'special advisors' of those in power.

They wrote an abundance of literature recording the poems, legends and myths of the culture and religion of past civilisations. This literary genre finds its examples in the story of the Jews, some of it in the Old Testament in the books of Job, Psalms, Proverbs and Ecclesiastes. Some scholars would also include the Song of Solomon.

1

Prologue: chapters 1—2

Have you considered my servant Job? There is no one on earth like him; he is blameless and upright, a man who fears God and shuns evil.

JOB 1:8

Start here: read chapters 1 and 2
- Job introduced
- Satan's challenge and Job's first test: note Job's response
- Satan's second challenge and Job's second test: note Job's response

The opening chapters introduce us to Job and set the story in a recognisably human context. They supply all the biographical detail about Job that is available to us. He lived in 'the land of Uz', which may have been in territory to the east of Jordan that became part of Edom, so not part of Israel. Job may not, then, have been an Israelite. He was known and respected beyond his own country for his wealth, his integrity and his faith. Job was a prosperous family man – all the numbers being suggestive of the ideal family and business (1:2-3).

The brief glimpse we are given of family life shows love and harmony between its members (1:4). Like the patriarchs, Job took spiritual responsibility for his family by acting as priest within the household, offering sacrifices against the possibility that his children had offended God during their partying (1:5).

So far, so good. This is what we might expect: the good and godly man is blessed with prosperity. Deuteronomy 28 predicts this and

Psalm 1 expects it – often, so do we. Indeed, some build a theology on this presupposition.

From this gentle, pastoral opening scene, we move into a sort of 'bifocal' view of Job's life: in one view, we see the disasters which fell upon him from the perspective of the man and his family, friends and employees; in the other view, we are taken behind the scenes, as it were, to see from the perspective of God and the spiritual realm. Here, a bigger picture is revealed than Job and his friends are ever able to see.

Having introduced us to the main character, the story moves from earth to wherever is meant by 'the presence of the Lord' (2:7; see also 1:6), which some take to be heaven. The location is, however, incidental; what matters is the occasion itself. A 'holy convocation' is in process at which 'angels', also described as 'sons of God' (literally 'the hosts'), present themselves before God. We are not told anything about the purpose of the occasion or whether it was a frequent gathering or something unusual. All we know is that in this instance, apparently exceptionally, Satan was also present, fulfilling his function as 'the adversary' – which is what his name means.

There follows an exchange between God and Satan – which, in itself, raises unanswerable questions. But it is made very clear that Satan is not God's equal in any way! God initiates the conversation. God points to the example of Job, giving the most remarkable testimonial imaginable, and then repeating it. This was an exceptional man: 'There is no one on earth like him' (1:8; 2:3). Satan, who is only ever responding to what God says, wants nothing more than to bring Job down. He knows that he cannot lay a finger on Job without God's permission. Satan completely misunderstands and misrepresents Job's goodness: he attributes Job's righteousness to self-interest. Take away his 'stuff' and, alleges Satan, Job will curse God. The implied wager is accepted by God in that he will allow Satan power to act against Job so long as the man himself is unharmed (1:12).

On a single day, when Job's children are together feasting, a series of disasters strikes Job's family. A messenger rushes into Job's office with news that two crucial herds – the oxen which did the ploughing and the donkeys which carried the produce – have been stolen by rustlers who then killed the herdsmen as well. There is no time to react before another messenger bursts in to report that a freak natural disaster has killed the whole of his vast flock of sheep and their shepherds. Still reeling from this news, Job's response is interrupted by the arrival of another distraught employee telling him that foreigners have stolen his 3,000-strong herd of camels and killed their keepers. With his business in tatters, Job has one more messenger who will give him the worst news yet: all his children have died under the sudden collapse of the building where they were partying.

Critically, the focus is now on Job: how will he respond? His agri-business is in ruins; many of his employees have been murdered; worst of all, the sons, who had probably worked with him in the family firm, were dead and his beautiful daughters too. Will Satan's prediction be fulfilled? Grief-stricken, Job falls to the ground – in worship! Such is his faith that he accepts the overwhelming pain and trusts in God's inscrutable wisdom. In the midst of his anguish, he recognises the goodness of God. To paraphrase: 'It was the Lord who gave; it was the Lord who removed; and in the Lord alone must the explanation of these strange happenings be sought.'[5] Yet this very faith does not relieve the pain; rather, it intensifies it.

For reflection: Job 1:21

Naked I came from my mother's womb,
    and naked I shall depart.
The Lord gave and the Lord has taken away;
    may the name of the Lord be praised.
JOB 1:21

Job's reaction to the devastating losses he suffered speaks powerfully to us in an age when we have so much stuff. There are times when Job seems so New Testament – which, given that both were inspired by the same Spirit, is not really surprising. Compare his comments on loss with remarks by Paul and James.

> Naked I came from my mother's womb,
>   and naked I shall depart.
> JOB 1:21

> For we brought nothing into the world, and we can take nothing out of it.
> 1 TIMOTHY 6:7

Of course, we know this: it is obvious. Every baby ever born came into the world with nothing but their amazingly compact self, humanity in so small and vulnerable a package. Before long, at least in developed countries, the power to acquire things shows itself, even if it is only by a process of point, scream and then suck. Soon the toy cupboard will be full and still the same method is employed, modified a little: point and pout. We go through life wanting, getting, scheming, collecting as we fill our homes and our hearts with more and more things.

'How much did he leave?' a relative asks the executor. 'Everything' is always the answer. It is a sobering thought and we do well to learn from Job. But how was he able to stand aside from his wealth in this way? He never lost sight of its source.

> The Lord gave and the Lord has taken away;
>   may the name of the Lord be praised.
> JOB 1:21

> Every good and perfect gift is from above, coming down from the Father of the heavenly lights, who does not change like shifting shadows.
> JAMES 1:17

All Job's prosperity was given to him. Of course, he had worked hard for it. He had a shrewd business brain, no doubt, and the help of his sons, but without God's giving there would have been no receiving. What an example to us this is.

Job passes the first test, demonstrating that God's assessment of him was correct: his trust in God was the expression of genuine love. Satan appears not in the least embarrassed by his exposure as a liar when he next appears in God's presence. He continues to argue that Job's faith is motivated solely by self-interest and that if God were to permit Satan to touch Job physically – in his body – then the man would certainly show that his faith was a sham. Satan makes a disturbingly realistic, though cynical, assessment of our priorities: 'A man will give all he has for his own life' (2:4). So, once again, in order to demonstrate that a person may love God for his own sake, God gives permission for Satan to do what he chooses so long as Job's life is spared (2:6).

The focus returns to the human level: Job's body becomes drenched in pain from a terrible skin condition. He retreats to the place for society's untouchables in deep humiliation and anguish. Although the physical impact is dreadful, the spiritual effect is far greater. Job believes in a just God who rewards righteousness and punishes sin. How, then, could this be happening to him when he has been meticulous in his personal holiness and religious practice?

Suffering is, of course, a problem to the sufferer, but its ripples touch other lives too, especially family and friends. Job's wife is also grief-stricken at the losses they have suffered and now she sees her only remaining strength and support devastated by a terrible and repugnant illness. Her outburst – 'Are you still maintaining your integrity? Curse God and die!' (2:9) – bespeaks her desperation: why not end it all by cursing God and being blasted by divine judgement? For Job, it is another layer to his agony, but he bows his head in acceptance of what God sends, and what a challenge is in that submission: 'Shall we accept good from God, and not trouble?' (2:10). It is a statement that could be the theme for the rest of the book. 'In all this, Job did not sin in what he said' (2:10; see also 1:22).

Bad news travels far and fast. Perhaps living far from Job, his friends hear of his plight and come together to visit him. Their attitudes and actions in making this response are movingly sensitive and supportive. What they find is far worse than they had imagined. Overcome with horror, grief and anger, they join him in the place of his humiliation. For seven days, they sit with him among the ashes of the community rubbish heap, silently sharing Job's anguish. We will note their failings in due course but at this point we can have nothing but praise for their deep empathy for their friend. When faced with tragedy and horror in the lives of friends, we feel completely inadequate to offer words of comfort and hope. For this reason, many remain at an embarrassed distance. Never underestimate the power of presence, even when it is wordless. An arm of support, shared tears, sighs and silent prayers do more to reach across the loneliness of pain to offer comfort than speeches that are barely audible to the sufferer.

Suffering is a universal human experience. Few, if any, pass through life without being touched by its tentacles in one way or another. We all find, sooner or later, that 'shadows fall on brightest hours, that thorns remain'.[6] Yet we, like Job, are surprised, perhaps angry, when it happens to us. Libraries could be filled with the books written about experiences of suffering or explanations or 'how to cope' manuals. Fortunes have been made by those offering solutions. The book of Job is neither a 'cure-all' nor about coping. It offers us three different responses to suffering which are as real and as relevant today as when it was first written.

The scene is now set against which the drama of the poem will be acted out across the chapters and the responses explored. The speakers will wrestle with this most profound of human challenges.

They will try to explain a cosmic drama in entirely terrestrial terms. Job understands that what is happening is the result of God's 'hidden hand', and that is what causes him such pain. He, like us, looks in vain for an explanation in his past; Job, and we, must learn that suffering may say more about the future than the past.

For you to consider

Paul encourages us to make an honest assessment of ourselves:

> Think of yourself with sober judgement, in accordance with the faith God has distributed to each of you.
> ROMANS 12:3

- God's assessment of Job was unequivocal: this was an exceptionally good man! What sort of statement might God be able to make about you? We are not expected to condemn ourselves but to acknowledge both our strengths and our weaknesses, our achievements and our failings. So, what about you?

- Consider where you are most vulnerable to temptation and failure in your Christian life. What can you do to forestall an attack by Satan?

- At first, the three friends visited Job but had nothing to say. What would you have done in that situation? Is there anyone you know who needs your presence at the moment?

Part I

The blame game
(chapters 3—27)

Consider now: who, being innocent, has ever perished?
JOB 4:7

How shall we describe the interchange between Job and his friends? It is neither a debate, nor an argument, nor a conversation. Yet it is more than an exchange of views, as the three friends try to persuade Job he is in the wrong, while he protests the injustice of his sufferings.

The form in which the exchange is reported is Hebrew poetry, from chapter 3 through to the beginning of the epilogue in chapter 42 (see box below). Like poetry in any language, the poetry in Job slows us down. It requires us to think more carefully about what we are reading. It is rich in metaphor and simile, expressing the everyday in graphic pictures. We have to pause and ponder from time to time. Wouldn't it be better for truth to be stated and explained plainly? Maybe, but the writer of Job aims for more than education. It is not only our reason that is the target but also our emotions. The writer wants to change the way we think about God, ourselves and suffering – and he wants to change the way we feel.

Hebrew poetry

Poetry is a form of writing that does not translate well from one language to another, or from one culture to another. English poetry relishes the sounds of its words as well as their graphic power and rhythm. Hebrew poetry was probably similarly concerned with the stress and rhythm of its words but, as much of that is lost in the mists of time, we cannot be sure how far this was the case. But it also has another distinctive feature: the carefully choreographed repetition of ideas and expression. This can be retained in translation even where the strongly rhythmic element may be lost.

Hebrew poetry is notable for its parallelism. This may simply be in the form of a restatement of one line using different words, or a second line may amplify the thought of the first. Sometimes the effect is achieved by way of contrast with a preceding line or by making the second line a more dramatic version of the first. We need to take a slower pace as we read. The opening verses of Job chapter 3 illustrate the style clearly:

> May the day of my birth perish
>   and the night that said, 'A boy is conceived!'
> That day – may it turn to darkness;
>   may God above not care about it;
>   may no light shine on it.
>
> JOB 3:3–4

2

Job's lament: chapter 3

Why is life given to a man
  whose way is hidden,
  whom God has hedged in?

JOB 3:23

Start here: read chapter 3
- Job wishes he had never been born
- Why, he asks, didn't I die at birth?
- Job questions his pointless existence

Job's three friends found themselves in a strange situation. They had come to comfort and support him, but day after day they sat among the stinking rubbish waiting for some indication of Job's response to what he was going through. They would have heard his sighs and his tears, and the shrieks of pain that may have accompanied the awful scraping of his sores to remove the foul-smelling pus. Perhaps Job's wife had told them how the last thing he had said to her (2:10) suggested that his faith in God held firm. Perhaps they discussed how they might respond to what Job might say, but until Job himself spoke they must wait. Finally, on the eighth day, he did speak, and from his mouth poured one of the saddest laments to be found in the whole of scripture.

After however long since his sufferings began, and after another seven long days in the burning heat of the sun, Job finally gives voice to suffering beyond the agony of his sores and his sickness. Acute suffering destroys a sense of perspective. It subverts every memory of good we have known. It becomes a distorting lens through which we view both past and present. Every good Job had enjoyed was now forgotten or dismissed as worthless.

For startling, shocking poetry, this lament is in a league of its own. Its theme was that age-old cry of a human being in pain – 'Why?' – but in its most hopeless form: 'Why was I ever born?' Any hope Job's friends had that his spirit was holding up well vanished before the first sentence had ended. Here was raw grief, anger and despair.

Job begins with curses, as one might expect, but not against the disasters but against his own birth. He wishes that it had never happened, had never brought joy or pride to his parents. Then this awful life he was living would never have had to begin (3:3–10).

There is only so much to be said by way of cursing and Job moves on to the inevitable next stage: why? How can there be any sense, any purpose to the life his had become? Stillbirth would have been preferable, opening the door to Sheol – the place of the departed. There he would be at peace as are all the dead, whether great or small, noble or ignoble (3:11–19).

Instead, he must endure the bitterness of living, where the only joy in life is in its ending. Job feels trapped, hedged in by God himself, filled with dread, unable to rest or to be at peace (3:20–26).

Acute suffering also challenges our expectations. Job's faith was in a God who is good, who rewards righteousness and punishes wickedness. And God is like that – but he is not only like that!

Coleridge once criticised Christians for believing not in God himself, but only in their beliefs about him. Great suffering puts an end to beliefs in beliefs.[7] The challenge for Job is to know that God is much more than he understands him to be. We may, like him, be disappointed with God when the God in whom we are disappointed is a figment of our imagination, a God made in our own image.

This is the difficult message of the book of Job: how do we reconcile what we believe about God with the sometimes bitter experience of living in a fallen world? Why, when we need him most, does God seem so distant? It is a theme that will develop as we proceed through the book, but at the outset some things are beginning to emerge. Here are four sages thinking deeply about suffering, yet they have no satisfactory answer. The reason? They have only partial information, or, as Paul wrote centuries later, they – like we – 'see through a glass, darkly' (1 Corinthians 13:12, KJV). It is like trying to view a 50-room mansion through a keyhole in the front door. All we can talk about when we try to explain God's actions is all we can see, when in fact there is far more to be known: more in what is past, more in the present and everything in the future – both of time and eternity.

Faith is never more challenged than in the face of suffering.

For reflection: which side of the hedge?

> Have you not put a hedge around him and his household and everything he has?
> JOB 1:10

> Why is life given to a man
>   whose way is hidden,
>   whom God has hedged in?
> JOB 3:23

Frustrated, Satan, complains to God, 'Have you not put a hedge around him?' (1:9–10). Satan wants to bring down Job but God has erected a Satan-proof fence around him so the devil could find no way through. We may smile at the picture of Satan slinking off with steam billowing from his ears. Satan would have to find another hedge to break through!

Without question, Satan is powerful, determined, devious, hostile and persistent. Peter referred to him as 'a roaring lion' (1 Peter 5:8) – from experience, perhaps? We may not have the reputation of a Job or a Peter but if the devil were to succeed in destroying our faith there would be derisive laughter in hell, but as he tries to do so he will find there is a hedge around us too. Here is the evidence:

> No temptation has overtaken you except what is common to mankind. And God is faithful; he will not let you be tempted beyond what you can bear. But when you are tempted, he will also provide a way out so that you can endure it.
> 1 CORINTHIANS 10:13

The temptation can be resisted. The lion is on the other side of the hedge! And in heaven, Jesus is praying for us as he prayed for Simon Peter (Luke 22:31–32; Hebrews 7:25).

However, every hedge has two sides; what was happening on Job's side? Job was also frustrated! He felt trapped: he couldn't escape what was happening to him (3:23). The flip side of Job's protection was prevention. He might have felt better if he could have discarded his reputed goodness. But that was not an option. Blessing has obligations. When Satan is hedged out, we are hedged in; Job is right. But that is not the whole story, as Paul told the Galatians:

> You, my brothers and sisters, were called to be free. But do not use your freedom to indulge the flesh; rather, serve one another humbly in love.
> GALATIANS 5:13

We are given a new liberty with new boundaries. The freedom God has given us has a hedge around it against our own sinful inclinations. It is as much a protection from ourselves as from Satan.

For you to consider

- You have probably been in a situation where a friend or family member has needed help to deal with suffering. How did you respond? What did you find most effective? Where could you have done better?

- Job is not the only Bible character to struggle with depression. Compare the experiences of Elijah (1 Kings 19:1–9) and Jeremiah (Jeremiah 20:14–18). Find similarities with and differences from Job's experience. Note any differences in the ways they responded.

- Suffering challenges us to think about our own expectations. If they have been based on our beliefs about God, do those beliefs have strong roots in the Bible? Are they more about our Christian culture than about scripture?

- The psalmist, David, suffered disappointment and seems to have battled with depression at times. Psalm 42 shows us how he dealt with it. How would you use this psalm to help a friend who is suffering?

- Who do you know who would benefit from a visit from you this week?

3

Job's comforters

When Job's three friends... heard about all the troubles that had come upon him, they set out from their homes and met together by agreement to go and sympathise with him and comfort him.
JOB 2:11

To describe someone as a 'Job's comforter' is hardly complimentary, but the bad press given to Job's friends is only partly justified: at least they were there for him when no one else was. This man, so accustomed to the bustle of his business and social responsibilities, must have felt very alone out there on the rubbish heap, with only the rats for company. If the three friends were disappointed by the lack of welcome, they were not without reason: their good intentions seem to have prompted not a word of appreciation from Job.

By the time we reach the end of the exchanges between Job and his friends, we may have developed a rather negative view of them and their attempt to comfort him. But these men come with a genuine concern for their friend and a real desire to support him in his suffering. They are deeply perplexed by the tragedy and want to find an explanation which will help Job find a pathway through his grief and loss to restoration and happiness once more. And now that they have heard Job's dark depression and the despair that has overwhelmed this man, once renowned for his faith, what will they say? What *can* they say?

We discover that they can and do have a lot to say. Three times Eliphaz speaks about his insight into the underlying cause and its solution, each time at considerable length. Bildad is less wordy and by his third speech he seems to have run out of ideas and patience. Zophar has even less to say and only manages two relatively short speeches.

One thread is common to them all, something that in the 21st century seems almost quaintly old-fashioned: they all believe we live in a moral universe, that there are moral absolutes. They believe that some things are right and some are wrong – always. It is a view found right through the Bible and indeed it was universally accepted across the centuries, only beginning to buckle under the pressure of what we call the Enlightenment, finally collapsing almost completely in the modern and postmodern atmosphere of the late 20th and early 21st centuries. So, we may find that we have to adjust our outlook if we are to come alongside Job and his friends and accept their premise that moral law is set not by public opinion but by the higher authority of divine revelation.

Let us listen to the three friends in turn and try to understand how well or otherwise their solutions fit Job's case. We will then be better placed to consider Job's response.

Eliphaz – the pastoral approach

The first speech: chapter 4 and 5

Start here: read chapters 4 and 5
- Eliphaz tentatively reminds Job how he has helped others
- The core of the argument (especially 4:8)
- Eliphaz has a personal revelation

The choice of Eliphaz to begin the contribution of the friends may have been determined by his seniority. Eliphaz is certainly the gentlest and most pastorally sensitive of the three and begins cautiously, even tentatively (4:2). He wants to remind his friend of the times when he himself has helped others and urges him to draw strength from the advice he has given (4:3–4).

With this brief lead-in, Eliphaz comes to the heart of his argument. He calls on Job to be reasonable: 'Consider now!' (4:7), and makes his pitch with a universal principle:

> Those who sow trouble reap it.
> JOB 4:8

Take note of this; it underlies almost everything Eliphaz will say and is echoed again and again by Bildad and Zophar. But, are they right?

Sowing and reaping are expressions of cause and effect, which are so much part of our everyday lives. God seems to follow this principle, blessing those who do right and judging those who do wrong. It was fundamental to the covenant relationship between God and Israel (Deuteronomy 28:1–2, 15).

This same message is found throughout the ministry of the prophets. They warn against impending judgement and call God's people to repentance. And we find it in the New Testament too. It is the principle which underlies the beatitudes in the sermon on the mount. Paul uses it as an incentive to practical Christian living:

> A man reaps what he sows. Whoever sows to please their flesh, from the flesh will reap destruction; whoever sows to please the Spirit, from the Spirit will reap eternal life.
> GALATIANS 6:7–8

So what is Eliphaz trying to say? Since God punishes sin and wrongdoing, and given that suffering is a punishment from God, then Job is obviously being punished for sin. He should repent and change his behaviour.

That is not a message Job is likely to welcome. How could Eliphaz make it more effective? His solution is to share a special word from God, a personal revelation that he has received for the benefit of his friend. He tells Job about a spine-tingling experience:

> A word was secretly brought to me…
> Amid disquieting dreams in the night,
>   when deep sleep falls on people,
> fear and trembling seized me
>   and made all my bones shake.
> A spirit glided past my face,
>   and the hair on my body stood on end.
> JOB 4:12–15

Then the spirit stopped and stood before him – and it spoke!

> I heard a hushed voice:
> 'Can a mortal be more righteous than God?
>   Can even a strong man be more pure than his Maker?'
> JOB 4:16–17

Even before Job can respond to Eliphaz's charge that God is punishing his sin, he is warned that God has to be right; God has sent a spirit to confirm the message. Job must admit that he has brought judgement on himself. So, man up, Job, and face the facts: God must be right!

As if this were not discouraging enough, Eliphaz bluntly tells Job that prayer is pointless while he is in his present state of mind (5:1). So, what should Job do, Eliphaz? You can't crush him like this and leave him with no way forward. Awkwardly, perhaps, he puts forward a course of action. It is well meant, without doubt, and what follows is sound advice:

> But if I were you, I would appeal to God;
>   I would lay my cause before him.
> JOB 5:8

In beautiful poetry, Eliphaz then speaks of God's grace in saving the needy and giving hope to the poor. Perhaps, Job, God is disciplining you. Though that may be hard to take, the result will be for your benefit:

> For he wounds, but he also binds up;
>   he injures, but his hands also heal.
> JOB 5:18

Eliphaz has spoken for the friends as well as himself (5:27). Job's failure to accept his line of argument requires the others also to speak, as we shall see shortly. But even when they have each spoken in the discussion, Job is unmoved. Their basic premise that he has brought his sufferings on himself is rejected out of hand.

For reflection: the value of discipline

> Blessed is the one whom God corrects;
>   so do not despise the discipline of the Almighty.
> JOB 5:17

God disciplines us! Some people react against the idea, regarding discipline as contrary to God's fatherly love. Some believe themselves to be under God's discipline. Over the years, I have known Christians who have persistent health problems – depression and back pain, in the cases which spring to mind – which they believe to be the result of their past sin or failure. It is the cross they have to bear. Both have misunderstood what the Bible teaches.

Eliphaz is correct in saying that God uses discipline in the lives of his children. There are several other references to this in the Bible, the most instructive of which comes in the letter to the Hebrews:

> Endure hardship as discipline; God is treating you as his children… God disciplines us for our good, in order that we may share in his holiness. No discipline seems pleasant at the time, but… it produces a harvest of righteousness and peace.
> HEBREWS 12:7, 10–11

The mistake that some make is to confuse discipline with punishment. Punishment is a form of retribution. Discipline is positive: it is a form of training, intended to teach us something. The suggestion that discipline takes the form of back pain, or depression, or that some persistent difficulty is God's payback for past sins, misunderstands forgiveness. It implies that we need to suffer because Christ's sufferings for us are not sufficient to deal with our failings. We may have to carry scars from our past but they should serve as reminders of God's grace rather than his grudge. Discipline is a sign of God's love (Psalm 94:12)!

God loves us as a father and, like any good father, wants the best for us. He wants us to be mature, rounded sons and daughters who 'share in his holiness'. For that to happen, some of our preferences have to be changed, our understanding developed, our self-centredness challenged; we have to see that there is a better way. Discipline makes that clear for us. It turns us on to the right path and trains us for the demands it makes on us. But it is worth it. 'Endure hardship as discipline' (Hebrews 12:7). When the going is tough, embrace it as an opportunity rather than complain about it. It is for your good. The goal makes it worthwhile:

> Everyone who competes in the games goes into strict training. They do it to get a crown that will not last; but we do it to get a crown that will last for ever.
>
> 1 CORINTHIANS 9:25

What Eliphaz says about discipline is true, affirmed in many other places in the Bible, and we do well to learn from it. But it just didn't explain what was happening to Job.

Discipline is an aspect of discipleship!

The second speech: chapter 15

Start here: read chapter 15
- Eliphaz dismisses Job's defence
- Why should God listen to Job?
- The wicked are always punished; they cannot prosper

Job responds at length, rejecting his friend's argument, so Bildad steps up to put forward a similar argument from a different perspective. Again, Job will have none of it, so Zophar follows but he too fails to change Job's outlook. With each reply, Job seems to be growing stronger in his rejection, which may explain the note of impatience and frustration in this second speech by Eliphaz.

The gloves are off this time. Eliphaz begins with an insult: 'You are an old windbag' might be a modern paraphrase (15:2)! He accuses Job of undermining the faith of others, of dishonesty and deceit (15:3–6). And his stubbornness is offensive (15:9).

> The grey-haired and the aged are on our side,
>   men even older than your father…
> Why has your heart carried you away,
>   and why do your eyes flash,
> so that you vent your rage against God?
> JOB 15:10, 12–13

'Wise men,' says Eliphaz, know that 'the wicked man suffers torment' (15:20).

The final section of the speech – again in graphic poetry – is, in effect, a restatement of the core argument that God punishes those who do wrong: what a person sows, they reap. It is obvious, says Eliphaz. You see it on every hand, he implies. If in the short-term the wicked seem to prosper, it cannot last.

> Though his face is covered with fat
>   and his waist bulges with flesh,
> he will inhabit ruined towns
>   and houses where no one lives…
> He will no longer be rich and his wealth will not endure…
>   the breath of God's mouth will carry him away.
> JOB 15:27–30

Case made; case closed! No, not yet, Eliphaz.

The third speech: chapter 22

Start here: read chapter 22
- Job has sinned – like this!
- God knows Job has sinned
- But there is hope if Job will own up

Once again, the same sequence follows: Job responds, then Bildad speaks followed by Job, and then Zophar again followed by Job. And still the outcome is the same: Job digs his heels in and refuses to accept their explanation of his suffering. Eliphaz makes one final attempt to make Job see the error of his ways. At first, he is quite brutal in his approach (22:3–5).

Out of nowhere, Eliphaz conjures up a list of 'crimes' with which he accuses his friend. He has been mean, heartless, cruel and unjust. His selfishness has caused untold suffering for those who are weak and defenceless: That is why 'snares are all around you' (22:10). Job won't get away with it (22:15–18)! It is the same 'sowing and reaping' argument in another guise.

Perhaps Eliphaz sees a pained look in Job's eyes, the drooping shoulders, and his tone seems suddenly to become more caring. Eliphaz makes a final plea with Job to 'submit to God and be at peace with him' (22:21). There is hope for those who will turn from their sinful ways:

> If you return to the Almighty, you will be restored…
> You will pray to him, and he will hear you.
> JOB 22:23, 27

True indeed and beautifully expressed, but to the end Eliphaz has failed to understand Job's problem or the cause of his grief, so even his best remedies do not bring relief. Eliphaz has offered such a high view of God that he has lost sight of grace and compassion.

Bildad – the scholarly approach

Eliphaz's failure to persuade Job must have been disappointing to his well-intentioned friends. The gentler pastoral approach of his first speech was, it seems, not the best strategy. Time for the 'big guns'.

Bildad's appeal to past scholarship suggests that he was, or aspired to be, well-versed in the intellectual consensus of his times. Philosophers in every age – like theologians – have wrestled with the issues of suffering and justice. Thinking people ask why our world is marked by disaster and pain. So we find ourselves asking, 'Why? Why do men fight wars when history shows how futile they are? Why is it the weak who are so often exploited? Why are the resources of the earth so unequally distributed? Why is there so much pain and sickness?' The disasters, the trauma, both natural and man-made, national and personal, are so numerous, so overwhelming – and seemingly so random, so pointless.

For some, the existence of suffering is sufficient to make them deny the existence of God. I cannot understand what help this is in addressing the questions. God or no God, there is still suffering to be faced. What possible comfort is there in atheism?

But let's get back to Bildad.

The first speech: chapter 8

Start here: read chapter 8
- Job's arguments are so much hot air
- God will listen if Job repents
- Scholarship and nature show Job is in the wrong

Bildad sees Job's rejection of Eliphaz' argument as tantamount to accusing God of injustice (8:3). That is obviously wrong on Job's part, so it is he who is mistaken. Bildad identifies Job's children as blameworthy (8:4). And, Job, since you claim to be innocent, you have only to ask God and he will put everything right again (8:5-6). This is not just simplistic; it is also cruel. Then, having laid the blame squarely on Job's family, Bildad launches into the philosophical basis for his conclusion. Again, the argument is in terms of cause and effect, with illustrations from the riverbank (8:8-19). Bildad advises his friend to trust in God; that way, he will be restored (8:20-21).

The second speech: chapter 18

Start here: read chapter 18
- Why do you treat us as fools, Job?
- Dreadful punishments fall on the ungodly in this life

Job is unmoved by Bildad's analysis and continues to reject it, so Bildad must return to the discussion to press home his point. His opening, 'Be sensible, and then we can talk' (18:2) sounds rather like, 'When will you see sense, Job? You're only making things worse for yourself' (18:4).

At this point, Bildad follows his friends by demonstrating that those who do evil are punished. It's a vivid poem, enough to send shivers down the spine of every sinner.

> The lamp of the wicked is snuffed out;
>   the lamp of his fire stops burning.
> Terrors startle him on every side…
> Calamity is hungry for him;
>   disaster is ready for him…
> It eats away parts of his skin.
> JOB 18:5, 11–13

It feels as if we are looking at one of those lurid medieval paintings depicting the horrors of hell, or an illustration from Dante's *Inferno*. We see the wicked man sitting in the dark (18:5-6), growing weaker (18:7), caught in a trap (18:8-10), terrified by the enveloping gloom (18:11), until finally the horror of it all destroys him (18:14). He is bereft of descendants (18:19), and even his name is forgotten (18:17).

Bildad knows that Job knows people of whom these things might be true. But it is not the whole truth, not by a long way!

The third speech: chapter 25

Start here: read chapter 25
- Be in awe of God
- 'Man is only a worm!'

By the time it is Bildad's turn to speak again, he has clearly run out of patience. Job has become more convinced that his own analysis is nearer the truth than are his friends' arguments. With one final, brief statement, Bildad's frustration and his true colours are revealed. If Job cannot be frightened into submission, then maybe he will respond to insults. The method is simple: set before him an awesome view of a remote, just God and bring out the huge contrast with this puny man – Job, of course – who has the audacity to suggest that his problems are all God's fault. So begin with God (25:2) and then contrast him with human beings (25:4). And then draw the obvious conclusion: 'a human being… is only a worm!'(25:6).

Job's response is heavy with irony:

> How you have helped the powerless!
>   How you have saved the arm that is feeble!
> What advice you have offered to one without wisdom!
>   And what great insight you have displayed!
> JOB 26:2-3

Like Eliphaz before him, Bildad has failed to meet Job where he really is… For Job, the questions are somewhere else. 'Why,' says Job, 'does your all-powerful God not come to me? Why does your God not deal justly with me?… Why do I not seem to matter any more?'

David Atkinson[8]

Zophar – the psychologist's approach

Zophar seems by far the least attractive of the three friends: 'a rather nasty piece of work'.[9] Certainly he does not project a great deal of warmth. Yet Zophar had shown deep concern for his friend Job. He had sat with him in the heat and stench of the rubbish tip, listened to his heart-rending cries and witnessed his pathetic suffering. But Zophar seems to have been the least moved by it – or perhaps he has just grown weary with Job's dogged refusal to accept sound advice.

Genuine counsellors and psychologists may be offended by my labelling Zophar as one of them; certainly, I have never met one who fell so far short of compassionate care. Perhaps I should describe him as an agony aunt of the 'pull-yourself-together' school of thought.

The first speech: chapter 11

Start here: read chapter 11
- This 'talker' – Job – must be challenged
- God is too great for us to understand his ways
- Job needs only to confess that he is in the wrong

From his opening words, Zophar shows himself impatient with Job's insistence that he is not guilty of the sins being attributed to him. 'Idle talk', he calls it, or 'babble' in some translations (11:3). Then, bluntly, he asserts that God has far more reason to punish Job than he is admitting (11:6). He has got off lightly so far!

Zophar then launches into a brief, impressive description of God's wisdom, but it is offered in a way that implies that this is something Job has failed to grasp whereas he, Zophar, has obviously understood it. It is but one example of how Zophar seems always to be talking down to Job. Now for some of Zophar's applied psychology:

> If [God] comes along and confines you in prison
>   and convenes a court, who can oppose him?
> Surely he recognises deceivers;
>   and when he sees evil, does he not take note?
> But the witless can no more become wise
>   than a wild donkey's colt can be born human.
>
> JOB 11:10–12

You get the implication, don't you? Job is the 'witless' or 'worthless' man here. He is the one who 'does not take note', who is incapable of learning his lesson. 'Yet,' Zophar says with flesh-creeping condescension, 'if you devote your heart to him' (11:13) – or to put it another way: if you take my advice – I can show you a sure-fire way out of your pain and suffering. Zophar has a simple four-step programme guaranteed to bring all the relief Job needs and every benefit he could desire! This is how it works:

> If you devote your heart to him,
>   and stretch out your hands to him,
> if you put away the sin that is in your hand
>   and allow no evil to dwell in your tent.
>
> JOB 11:13–14

The benefits that follow will resolve all Job's problems (11:15–19)! But if you don't accept this advice, Job, be warned:

> The eyes of the wicked will fail,
>   and escape will elude them;
>   their hope will become a dying gasp.
>
> JOB 11:20

With friends like that…!

How would you respond to Zophar? There is something appealing in his simple remedy. You can imagine the four steps printed on one side of a wallet card with the benefits on the reverse. All it required was for Job to get off his high horse and stop protesting his innocence. But put yourself in his position: the problems you have, the sufferings that are all too familiar, can all be gone in a moment! Wouldn't you want that, to walk in the sunny uplands of spiritual joy, health and prosperity? All you have to do is admit that you brought all these nasty things on your own head – the cancer, the redundancy, the misdemeanours of your teenagers, whatever. No problem then! Not unless it is not really like that, that your past has been a genuine attempt to know and serve God, to be a strength and blessing to those around you. The steps Zophar proposes are simple enough, but if they bear no relationship to the issues you face, how can they be expected to help? They belong to someone else's experience and needs, not yours. And not Job's either.

Which is exactly what Job felt:

> Doubtless you are the only people who matter,
>   and wisdom will die with you!
> But I have a mind as well as you.
> JOB 12:2–3

In fact, he goes further, suggesting that even animals and birds know better than Zophar (12:7).

The second speech: chapter 20

Start here: read chapter 20
- Zophar is offended by Job's rejection of his counsel
- The proud and wicked are snuffed out, Job is warned
- There is no benefit from wickedness, only distress

Zophar was offended at Job's rebuttal of his advice but he is still riding high, confident of his superior insight into his friend's troubles, and still offering the same failed explanation. Job must understand that those who live ungodly lives will suffer for it. Once more in graphic verse, Zophar paints a frightening picture of their fate.

> Though the pride of a godless person reaches to the heavens
>   and his head touches the clouds,
> he will perish forever, like his own dung;
>   those who have seen him will say, 'Where is he?'
> Like a dream he flies away, no more to be found.
>
> JOB 20:6–8

No matter that he disguises his wickedness, he will be exposed (20:12–14) and his end will be terrible:

> Surely he will have no respite from his craving;
>   he cannot save himself by his treasure…
> When he has filled his belly,
>   God will vent his burning anger upon him.
>
> JOB 20:20, 23

What has all this to do with the righteous Job? Well, that's just the point Zophar is trying to make: Job's sufferings are evidence that God is punishing him for his UNrighteousness! It's that old sowing and reaping theme again.

Zophar does not repeat his call to Job to repent. Nor does Zophar come back for a third speech, as do Eliphaz and Bildad. Some commentators think that in fact the speech he made has been mistakenly included in one by Job (27:13–23). That passage certainly has a similar tone to Zophar, but others explain that Job is possibly indulging in a sarcastic replaying of Zophar's message.

For you to consider

Before we analyse the weaknesses in the arguments of Job's friends, take some time to think about your own response to them. Remember their intention was to help Job find his way through his traumatic experiences.

- Do you have any experience of being comforted simply by the presence of supportive friends or family? What was it about that experience that you can draw upon to support someone else?

- What is it about suffering that makes us look for explanations in a person's character or past behaviour?

- Given their shared conviction as to the cause of Job's suffering, do you think his friends could have been more successful in helping him had they presented their case differently? Were they right in suggesting that his sufferings were evidence of sin on the basis of the sowing/reaping principle?

- The blame game has been shown to hinder development of good practice in many different settings. How important is it to identify our own responsibility when things go wrong?

Why did they fail?

The three friends set out to sympathise with and comfort Job (2:11). They failed in spite of being sincere and well-intentioned men, prepared to share as far as possible the discomfort and shame of Job's suffering. For this, they are to be admired; we can learn from them in this. We cannot begin to help the sufferers in our circle of acquaintance unless we are willing, as far as possible, to sit where they sit and feel what they feel. And scripture obliges us to do this.

> Weep with those who weep.
> ROMANS 12:15 (RSV)

> Carry each other's burdens, and in this way you will fulfil the law of Christ.
> GALATIANS 6:2

The problem we have with these three friends, however, is not so much with what they did or did not do; it is with what they said. They misunderstood God's ways and Job's needs. Consequently, they increased his pain rather than easing it. We need to learn from their mistakes.

Saying what is true is not the same as speaking the truth

At times, what they say seems to be wrong – but we can't fault it! Their theology seems spot-on, but their application of it isn't. For example, when they say that God blesses obedience, we know that is true; but they also seem to suggest that God operates at the level of a slot-machine. I put in my good deed for the day; God dispenses a blessing. God is not to be manipulated into doing exactly what we want him to do by our compliance with his rules, not a God who responds to lever-pulling faith – I say the right number of prayers, read the right amount of the Bible, put the right amount of money in the collection, or whatever – and, hey presto, God will comply with my demands, and thus give me a good life. That is not biblical religion.

We are moved by the eloquence of their speeches, by powerful theology or poetic beauty, but somehow, we know that they are answering the wrong questions. We have seen behind the scenes; we know the real reason for Job's troubles. He and his friends are never given this perspective. And because that perspective is unimaginable, its possibility is never taken into account by them or by Job. What they say may be true in itself, but it does not describe the truth of what is happening or its causes.

When Paul reminds us that we 'know in part' (1 Corinthians 13:12), we should take note. The three friends lacked the humility to acknowledge this, calling on personal revelation and scholarship to back up their ignorance. We should tread gently as we step into the sick room or sit by a distraught friend. We need to be honest enough to recognise how limited is our knowledge of them, of their situation, of their pain. We know even less about their heart before God.

The difference between what is true and what is the truth has everything to do with what may be really happening, which may be very different from what seems to us to be happening. We may too quickly assume causes from effect. We may know what is true in terms of doctrine but our application of it may be wrong – and thus is not the truth.

———————————————)X(———————————————

For reflection: what is truth?

This was not a novel question when Pilate asked it of Jesus. It is one that has challenged thoughtful people for much of human existence. One might have expected that by now it would have been settled, but it is one of the most important questions facing contemporary society. Let me explain, and then link back to Job and his friends.

'Post-truth' was identified as 'the word of the year' for 2016 by the Oxford English Dictionary. The fact that most of us, myself included, had never heard the word before was irrelevant; it had gained status in the media. It reflected a worrying attitude to truth.

Post-truth is used when facts are less influential than emotion. Facts can be rejected or ignored if they do not fit with the way a person feels about an issue. This was evident in the 2016 campaign leading up to the referendum about the UK's membership of the European Union. Both sides in the campaign were presenting 'facts' which had little bearing on the outcome because the mood generated by the campaigners was much more powerful. Then, in January 2017, Donald Trump was inaugurated as President of the United States of America. The following day we heard him attack the media for allegedly understating attendance at the ceremony, in spite of photographic evidence which clearly showed that it was not the largest ever. It was an example of post-truth, with the President exonerating himself on the basis of 'alternative facts'. Facts and emotion collided.

Time was when 'truth' could be regarded as something objective. It was not a matter of what I thought, felt, wanted or preferred: it was there, a fact with its place in time and space because of revelation, historical event, scientific discovery or whatever. It was what Francis Schaeffer called 'true truth'. This objectivity was challenged when, following the Enlightenment, human reason was given authority alongside revelation, until in the 20th century postmodernism made truth relative, a personal matter. It allowed me to have my truth and you to have your truth, even if the two were contradictory. I could be right and you could be right – no matter that we both might be completely at odds with facts and reality.

Does it matter? Yes, it does. The wonder of the gospel of Jesus is that it is rooted in history and grounded in real space-time events. That is what makes it unique in world religions. It presents us with the fact that God came personally into the world as a real human being who lived in a particular geographical location at a specific time in history and experienced the range of human life and death. It is this that makes Jesus so relevant to me and to every other human being. The gospel speaks what is true about the human condition and offers a credible answer to our deepest needs.

So what has this to do with Job's friends and their argument? Their failure was to face the facts about Job's life. They were emotionally committed to an explanation that simply did not sit true to the life story of the man they knew. They found themselves concocting accusations of immoral and inhuman behaviour in an attempt to justify their conviction. Post-truth rules OK – hundreds of years before Christ!

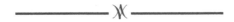

Quoting the Bible is not the same as thinking biblically

Some people say, cynically, that you can prove anything from the Bible! That is obviously false, but we are very prone to making it say what we like to hear. Job's friends don't actually quote the Bible at Job – that would hardly have been possible – but they do say things we find familiar because they appear elsewhere in scripture. When Eliphaz tells Job: 'Those who sow trouble reap it' (4:8), his words fit exactly with what Paul wrote centuries later: 'A man reaps what he sows' (Galatians 6:7). Moses issued a warning in the same vein when he says, 'Be sure that your sin will find you out' (Numbers 32:23). Scripture and logic agree. But Job rejects the argument that his friends base on this principle, though they put it repeatedly in a variety of ways. Is he right to do so?

What are the friends saying by insisting on this line of argument? They affirm that sin will be punished by God; that is self-evident because God is just. They also affirm that God uses suffering and pain as instruments of his judgement and that God gives blessing to those who live righteously. The blessings may take the form of happy families, success, health and prosperity (see Deuteronomy 28). Eliphaz and his friends interpret Job's sufferings as evidence of God's judgement and they draw the obvious (to them) conclusion that Job must be guilty of sins which warrant God's punishment. Sowing and reaping in practice! But they are wrong.

If you decide to grow salad crops in your garden, you will need to prepare the ground, buy good seed and sow according to the instructions on the packet. You can then sit back as God will 'give the increase'. (Who said gardening isn't easy?) In a few weeks, given the right growing conditions and not too many slugs, snails, pigeons and squirrels, you can look forward to harvesting fresh lettuce and radish for your table. Sowing and reaping works! But what is this bright yellow flower floating above the lettuce seedlings? You didn't sow dandelions at the same time, did you? Of course not; but in your carefully prepared seed-bed, there were already thousands of tiny seeds waiting for the trigger you have provided to set them germinating. You find yourself reaping what you did not sow.

Do you now see the mistake that Job's friends were making? They were taking a principle that was true without recognising that it only works one way, from cause to effect. It may not work in reverse, and in Job's case it certainly did not. The principle was true but their conclusion was not the truth.

We, like them, may use the Bible to say what is true but it may not be the truth. Consider one or two examples. The Bible shows us that Jesus sets us a good example of how we should live. His compassion, his goodness, his integrity, his self-sacrifice, his opposition to injustice – at every point, he is someone worth following. But this is not the whole truth. To say that Jesus is a good example would find the support of the vast majority of people. They will happily include him in a pantheon of great men and women such as Florence Nightingale, William Wilberforce, Gandhi, Nelson Mandela, Mother Teresa and so on. But the Bible is saying more than this: it says that Jesus came to be our Saviour, the unique God-man, who gave his life for our salvation. Yes, it is true that he is our example and we may try to follow him as our example, but if we fail also to trust him as our Saviour, we miss the very reason for his coming into the world.

Or think about this matter of prosperity that was so significant to Job and his friends. The Old Testament promises those who obey God's law that they will be blessed with prosperity. Good people will receive good things. The old covenant operated very much as a physical kingdom where the evidence of God's favour took a primarily material form. When people today try to apply those same promises in physical terms, they find themselves disappointed and blame lack of faith on their part or accuse God of not keeping his word. They miss the fact that, in the era of the new covenant, we belong to a spiritual kingdom where God's blessings are primarily spiritual in nature and eternal in duration. The truth is that the Jesus we follow had 'nowhere to lay his head' (Luke 9:58) and when he died owned only the clothes he was wearing. He teaches us to 'seek first the kingdom and his righteousness' (Matthew 6:33).

When we want to comfort or encourage friends who are suffering, the Bible is a rich source of help, but choose with care how you draw from its well. A Christian leader tells how, when his wife was suffering depression, a friend visited to comfort and encourage her. As she left, she went out via the kitchen, passing a sink piled high with dirty dishes. She left a note on the window sill above the sink: 'I can do all things through him who gives me strength' (Philippians 4:13). To the depressed housewife, it was devastatingly judgemental of her weak faith! Could the friend not have paused long enough to do the washing up?

Loving involves listening

Job's friends showed their love by spending so much time with him and thinking so deeply about his pain, but they loved him on their own terms. It fell far short of what Job needed because it was not unconditional. You feel this as the debate proceeds: their concern for Job cools and their criticism becomes sharper. All they heard him say was by way of rejection of their arguments and what they implied. They failed to hear his bewilderment that they should now accuse him whom once they admired for uprightness. They did not hear his anguish as he felt that the God he loved and served had abandoned him, the friends he had were deserting him and the people he had helped were humiliating him. They were not listening. Had they been listening, his friends might have thought to remind Job that God had not deserted him, even if he had stepped back a little from the closeness which Job so much treasured. They might have told him that God hears our sighs and counts our tears.

Modern psychology has rediscovered wisdom that Jesus knew – that listening is all-important in effective counselling. Time and again, when Jesus met people he seemed to miss the point of their questions by addressing other issues. Nicodemus seems curious about miracles; Jesus talks to him about being born from above. The woman at the well seems bent on arguing about national religions; Jesus talks about the water of life. The paralysed man wants healing; Jesus talks about forgiveness. Superficially, Jesus seems not to be listening, but there has never been a better listener – because he hears the question of the heart, the longing that cannot express itself (John 2:25).

Let Jesus be our example when we would help people in pain. It may be that what they say points us in the wrong direction as they explain their emotions or describe their situation. What they are telling us may be distorted by their fear, twisted by their pain, reality made incoherent by the bewildering sense that they have lost God's presence and smile. Our part is to be that presence and to reflect that smile, to listen beyond the hurt and understand the longing for comfort.

It seems to be part of our psyche that we have to have an explanation for everything. We need to find a reason for our depression, the economic collapse, the outbreak of rioting – on and on, from the national to the personal, right down to the mundane: 'What did I eat that gave me indigestion?' And the purpose of all this probing is to find a cause and lay the blame on something or someone. The blame game has become deeply embedded in our culture, for good and ill. So let's not be too hard on the three friends; they were doing what we all do. But looking into the past is not the only way to understand what is happening in the present. We know, as they did not, that what was happening had little or nothing to do with Job's past. He really had been the man of exemplary behaviour he claimed to be. So, could the explanation lie in the future instead? Could there be another explanation altogether?

4

Job answers his friends

Start here
- Job's response to Eliphaz: read chapters 6—7, 16—17, 23—24
- Job's response to Bildad: read chapters 9—10, 19, 26
- Job's response to Zophar: read chapters 12—14, 21

How alone Job must have felt, weighed down with the appalling sadness of the death of ten children and any number of employees, an outcast from his own community and with even his own wife struggling with the horror of the disease that had afflicted him. What it must have meant to Job to see his friends arrive that first day! There was nothing the friends could do to alleviate his pain, mitigate his humiliation or reverse his loss. But they were there, lifting the fog of loneliness that had enveloped him. Even so, by the end of the first week of silence, he might have been disappointed that they had nothing to say. By the end of the following week, when, perhaps, the speeches had ended, Job might have wished that they had stayed silent after all!

Job certainly has a lot to say for himself, which is not surprising. After all, he is the one who is suffering and, whereas others might like to know why he is suffering, Job *needs* to know. And he has to do a lot of listening too, as his friends tell him where he has gone wrong and what he needs to do to put things right. Given that, in Job's opinion, they have completely misread the situation, he is determined to speak up for himself and correct their falsehoods. But there is more than self-justification here. He too explores the implications of what has happened to him and his family, wrestling with the facts as he knows them, trying to square them with his deeply held faith.

Not only does Job's understanding of his experience change, but he changes too. From the tragic figure of chapter 3, he grows into the defiant man of chapter 27. Job responds to each of the friends' speeches in turn; there is some repetition, but themes are developed as the argument proceeds. Let us look at some of those themes.

The issue of Job's suffering

Sickness and suffering are not necessarily the same thing. It may be possible for the nature of the disease to be identified and explained. Suffering is less easily explained; often it mystifies us, disturbs us, even frightens us. The three friends have a solution: it is a one-size-fits-all explanation, with all the inherent weaknesses in that approach. Job is not so much concerned with 'the problem of suffering'; his issue is the problem of *my* suffering. Why is this happening – to me, now? It is the first thing he says by way of response to Eliphaz' opening speech:

> If only my anguish could be weighed
>   and all my misery be placed on the scales!
> It would surely outweigh the sand of the seas –
>   no wonder my words have been impetuous.
> The arrows of the Almighty are in me,
>   my spirit drinks in their poison;
>   God's terrors are marshalled against me.
> JOB 6:2–4

This is not a passing, short-term illness that Job is going through which can be eased by a few choice words from Eliphaz and his friends. No, says Job, this has been going on for some time already. It is awful and shows no signs of improving: 'I have been allotted months of futility' (7:3). Life seems to be passing him by.

> My days are swifter than a weaver's shuttle,
>   and they come to an end without hope…
> The eye that now sees me will see me no longer;

you will look for me, but I will be no more.
As a cloud vanishes and is gone,
   so he who goes down to the grave does not return.
JOB 7:6, 8–9

My days are swifter than a runner;
   they fly away without a glimpse of joy.
They skim past like boats of papyrus,
   like eagles sweeping down on their prey.
JOB 9:25–26

And the nights are no better than the days.

When I lie down I think, 'How long before I get up?'
   The night drags on, and I toss till dawn…
When I think my bed will comfort me
   and my couch will ease my complaint,
even then you frighten me with dreams
   and terrify me with visions,
so that I prefer strangling and death,
   rather than this body of mine.
JOB 7:4, 13–15

Job's friends had witnessed his physical suffering. He was so different from the man they knew that he was barely recognisable (2:12). They had watched him scraping pus and maggots from his flesh with the crudest of surgical implements: shards of broken pottery. They had seen him weep until his eyes were red and swollen. Yet somehow, they could still point the finger, still lay the blame at his door and tell him that he had brought this on himself. We sense the sadness, the sense of unfairness Job feels that friends could treat him like this. There was also the humiliation:

I have become a laughing-stock to my friends…
   a mere laughing-stock, though righteous and blameless!
JOB 12:4–5

In a later speech, Job goes into more detail about the social impact of his experience. All his relationships have been affected so that even people who were dependent on him now reject him. And he holds God responsible!

> He has alienated my family from me;
>   my acquaintances are completely estranged from me.
> My relatives have gone away;
>   my closest friends have forgotten me…
> My breath is offensive to my wife;
>   I am loathsome to my own family.
> Even the little boys scorn me;
>   when I appear, they ridicule me.
> All my intimate friends detest me;
>   those I love have turned against me.
>
> JOB 19:13–14, 17–19

But Job rejects the argument that his sufferings are punishment for his failure because that is so obviously wrong.

> Why do the wicked live on,
>   growing old and increasing in power?
> They see their children established around them,
>   their offspring before their eyes.
> Their homes are safe and free from fear;
>   the rod of God is not on them…
> They spend their years in prosperity
>   and go down to the grave in peace.
> Yet they say to God, 'Leave us alone!
>   We have no desire to know your ways…'
> Have you never questioned those who travel?
>   Have you paid no regard to their accounts –
> that the wicked are spared from the day of calamity,
>   that they are delivered from the day of wrath?
>
> JOB 21:7–9, 13–14, 29–30

Making the connection from sin to suffering in the way Job's friends did may be morally satisfying to us, but it is not the way the world works. Yes, it was as the result of sin, the failure of Adam and Eve, acting as representatives of the human race, that pain and hardship entered the world. As a result of their sin, 'creation groans', dislocated from the perfect original that God made. And sometimes there is a connection between our sufferings and our sins; but the issues are more complex than this simplistic explanation.

The failure of friendship

Job's social circle shrank to almost nothing because, like the three friends, his community concluded that he was blameworthy. Sowing and reaping was the currency of their response too. Even those who were not close to him could see he must be guilty on the basis of 'no smoke without fire'. It could be that their ignorance of the person he was made their response understandable, if not excusable.

Job is quite clear about them:

> Anyone who withholds kindness from a friend
>   forsakes the fear of the Almighty.
> JOB 6:14

He tells them that he would have responded differently had their roles been reversed. Instead, he found them disappointing.

> But my brothers are as undependable as intermittent streams,
>   as the streams that overflow
> when darkened by thawing ice
>   and swollen with melting snow,
> but that stop flowing in the dry season,
>   and in the heat vanish from their channels…
> Now you too have proved to be of no help.
> JOB 6:15–17, 21

Job had once been regarded as a wise man, consulted by others for his insights, but now his friends speak to him as if he were a fool (13:2–9).

Far from softening their criticism of Job, the friends resort to 'fake facts' to make their point more strongly still, and Job becomes still more scathing of their efforts.

> How long will you torment me
>   and crush me with words?
> Ten times now you have reproached me;
>   shamelessly you attack me…
> Why do you pursue me as God does?
>   Will you never get enough of my flesh?
> JOB 19:2–3, 22

Job's final response to his friends drips with scathing irony.

> How you have helped the powerless!
>   How you have saved the arm that is feeble!
> What advice you have offered to one without wisdom!
>   And what great insight you have displayed!
> Who has helped you utter these words?
>   And whose spirit spoke from your mouth?
> JOB 26:2–4

It is too easy to join the party and speak of the utter failure of the friends to bring hope and help to Job without recognising that their failure could so easily be our failure next time we are faced with a person who is in deep trouble, whose problems seem to us to be, at least in part, self-inflicted. It may be that a person faces problems because they have risked their own well-being through indulgence in food or drink or drugs or sex or whatever – or so it may seem to the outsider. It is not our duty to shine a light on their faults and failings, to tell them to take responsibility, to mock their plight or challenge their wrong-doing, not when they are crushed by the weight of their pain or grief or self-doubt. Job's friends failed him because they lacked sensitivity. Their enthusiasm to prove that their own analysis was the right one was short-sighted. Jesus was by no means a soft touch, but he did not break the bruised reed or snuff out the smouldering wick (Matthew 12:20). Nor should we; rather, we should step gently through other peoples' sufferings.

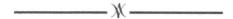

For reflection: Job 6:14

Anyone who withholds kindness from a friend forsakes the fear of the Almighty.

JOB 6:14

We are surrounded by people who are suffering. Illness and suffering are never purely personal. It touches the lives of other people, whether they are family, friends, neighbours, work colleagues or fellow members of the clubs, societies and churches to which each 'sufferer' belongs. It will affect us all, sooner or later. Like Job's friends, we will be expected to respond, but how? One of the challenging lessons to learn from the story of Job is that the response of others can profoundly affect the recovery – or continued suffering – of the other person.

There is, however, one way to avoid this: simply don't get involved! Being with people who are suffering is rarely a comfortable experience and we might make things worse rather than better. Leave it to those who are better placed to give the sort of support that the person needs; just 'walk by on the other side'. This familiar phrase comes from the parable of the good Samaritan (Luke 10:25–37). Jesus told how a traveller was mugged, robbed and left helpless on the roadside. First a priest and then a Levite who were also travelling on that road saw the man lying in the road, but each of them skirted round and went on their way, choosing not to get involved. It was a foreigner – a despised Samaritan – who, when he saw the man, looked after him and provided for his recovery. But do you remember why Jesus told the story?

By telling the story, Jesus made it clear that those who claim to love God are expected to love others on the basis of their need, not just because of family ties, shared faith or nationality or another presumed bond. The Christian is under obligation to help those who suffer who come within our orbit.

While becoming a Christian is personal, *being* a Christian is something more. We become part of a bigger family, the family of God; we become part of another body, the body of Christ. Each congregation of believers in Jesus is an expression of that bigger family, the body of Christ in miniature, as it were.

> God has put the body together, giving greater honour to the parts that lacked it… If one part suffers, every part suffers with it; if one part is honoured, every part rejoices with it.
> 1 CORINTHIANS 12:24–26

Mutual support within the Christian family becomes more than a duty; it is an expression of love. The same point is made in a different way, and even more strongly, by John.

> This is how we know what love is: Jesus Christ laid down his life for us. And we ought to lay down our lives for our brothers and sisters. If anyone has material possessions and sees a brother or sister in need but has no pity on them, how can the love of God be in that person? Dear children, let us not love with words or speech but with actions and in truth.
> 1 JOHN 3:16–18

> For whoever does not love their brother and sister, whom they have seen, cannot love God, whom they have not seen.
> 1 JOHN 4:20

This theme of mutual care and support runs through the letters written by Paul as well.

> Carry each other's burdens, and in this way you will fulfil the law of Christ.
> GALATIANS 6:2

Paul often ends his letters by offering encouragement to those who are helpers or those needing help. Some Christians seem to have greater spiritual stamina, while others need their fellow believers to rally round. Sharing the load, Paul says, is what Jesus expects of us.

> Therefore, as God's chosen people, holy and dearly loved, clothe yourselves with compassion, kindness, humility, gentleness and patience. Bear with each other.
> COLOSSIANS 3:12–13

> Encourage one another and build each other up, just as in fact you are doing.
> 1 THESSALONIANS 5:11

It would be wrong to imply that the only people for whom we feel concern are other believers. That would miss an important element of what we learn from the parable of the good Samaritan. There are people in need around us who make no pretence of faith but who also need our help, love and support. We must not become so obsessed with our own concerns that we fail to respond to those outside the circle of church life. The church in Galatia had become fixated on the finer points of theology so Paul wrote to them urging them to look around them.

> As we have opportunity, let us do good to all people, especially to those who belong to the family of believers.
> GALATIANS 6:10

Where is God in all this?

At first, Job seems almost apologetic when he responds to Eliphaz: 'Would I lie to your face?' (6:28), but as the discussion proceeds, he realises that he knows what they do not: he really has been careful to live uprightly; he has not brought judgement on himself. The more his friends accuse, the stronger becomes his conviction that there must be another explanation. But if his suffering is not self-inflicted, what other possibility is there? He can barely bring himself to put it into words; he would rather die!

> Oh, that I would have my request…
> that God would be willing to crush me,
>   to let loose his hand and cut off my life!
> Then I would have this consolation –
>   my joy in unrelenting pain –
>   that I had not denied the words of the Holy One.
> JOB 6:8–10

Perhaps then God would leave him alone and just let Job get on with bearing his punishment. After all, why should God be concerned with someone so insignificant, so far from perfect? He seems to quote the psalmist (or is the psalmist quoting Job?) who wrote:

> What is mankind that you are mindful of them,
>   human beings that you care for them?
> PSALM 8:4

But Job expresses a darker side of the same thought:

> What is mankind that you make so much of them,
>   that you give them so much attention,
> that you examine them every morning
>   and test them every moment?
> Will you never look away from me,

   or let me alone for an instant?
If I have sinned, what have I done to you,
   you who see everything we do?
Why have you made me your target?
   Have I become a burden to you?
JOB 7:17–20

From Job's perspective, it is a hopeless situation. How can he ever contest the superior wisdom of God?

How can I dispute with him?
   How can I find words to argue with him?
Though I were innocent, I could not answer him;
   I could only plead with my Judge for mercy.
Even if I summoned him and he responded,
   I do not believe he would give me a hearing.
He would crush me with a storm
   and multiply my wounds for no reason.
He would not let me catch my breath
   but would overwhelm me with misery.
If it is a matter of strength, he is mighty!
   And if it is a matter of justice, who can challenge him?
JOB 9:14–19

Yet it is a discussion that Job must have because, as he thinks further on his situation, he realises that the 'blame' for his sufferings is not his but God's!

But ask the animals, and they will teach you,
   or the birds of the earth, and they will tell you;
or speak to the earth, and it will teach you,
   or let the fish of the sea inform you.
Which of all these does not know
   that the hand of the Lord has done this?
JOB 12:7–9

It will be an unequal struggle:

> But I desire to speak to the Almighty
>   and to argue my case with God.
> JOB 13:3

If only he felt up to such a confrontation! The emotional toll of what he had suffered has been profound. He compares it with the way water wears down stone and washes away the soil (14:18–19). But his integrity is at stake; he cannot allow himself to be overwhelmed. He must know where he has gone wrong, why this dreadful fate has befallen him. He has looked deeply within himself and can find no explanation; he does not deserve all that has happened – and he needs to explain this to God! So far, he has tried and failed.

> Though I cry, 'Violence!' I get no response;
>   though I call for help, there is no justice.
> JOB 19:7

Job even questions why God does not have an appointment system!

> Why does the Almighty not set times for judgement?
> JOB 24:1

Who has not felt as Job felt at some stage? The sense of hopelessness before forces that are so much greater than ourselves, of being overwhelmed by circumstances beyond our control and crying out in the darkness for an explanation. The degree of Job's sufferings may be greater by far than anything we have known, but the bewilderment, the frustration, the sense of helplessness – all of this is familiar, is it not? Job senses that things could be different if only he had help, which was not available to him but has become available to us!

The need for a go-between

Early on in the discussion, Job has a thought which flickers for a moment and then is gone.

[God] is not a mere mortal like me that I might answer him,
   that we might confront each other in court.
If only there were someone to mediate between us,
   someone to bring us together,
someone to remove God's rod from me,
   so that his terror would frighten me no more.
Then I would speak up without fear of him,
   but as it now stands with me, I cannot.
JOB 9:32–35

The idea returns, again briefly but more brightly this time.

Even now my witness is in heaven;
   my advocate is on high.
My intercessor is my friend
   as my eyes pour out tears to God;
on behalf of a man he pleads with God
   as a man pleads for his friend.
JOB 16:19–21

The first thought was for arbitration that would ease Job's sufferings; the second was for someone to plead with God for mercy on Job. When the theme recurs for the third time, Job is beyond wishful thinking. He is making demands, wanting his view of his plight to be recorded as a permanent record, carved in stone as well as written on perishable vellum.

Oh, that my words were recorded,
   that they were written on a scroll,
that they were inscribed with an iron tool on lead,
   or engraved in rock for ever!

I know that my redeemer lives,
  and that in the end he will stand upon the earth.
After my skin has been destroyed,
  yet in my flesh I will see God;
I myself will see him
  with my own eyes – I, and not another.
  How my heart yearns within me.

JOB 19:23–27

It is as if Job has a moment of inspiration, a lightning flash of revelation in which he sees God as his redeemer, the one who has bought freedom. And in that moment, Job knows that he has a future, whatever the course of his dreadful disease. He will see God. It is an incredible vision which runs directly counter to the expectation of life after death of his contemporaries. He glimpses something more than *Sheol*, the place of shadows where the dead were believed to dwell. This is something more New Testament, a resurrection into the conscious presence of God. But, as the moments after the lightning flash make the darkness seem even darker, so he is plunged into gloom again: 'How my heart yearns within me!' Yet something lingers of the realisation he has been given. The searching for God is renewed, the longing for fellowship with him is fortified, the hope that God will hear is strengthened.

But he knows the way that I take;
  when he has tested me, I will come forth as gold.
My feet have closely followed his steps;
  I have kept to his way without turning aside.
I have not departed from the commands of his lips;
  I have treasured the words of his mouth more than my daily
  bread.

JOB 23:10–12

He has not found an answer for his sufferings, for that is not what the book is really about, but it has brought him nearer to understanding what God is like. It is not what he expected!

Job does not tell us what he would look for in a go-between, but we can guess. He will need to be God-like, to have the very qualities which Job found so daunting about God. He must be holy enough to stand in God's presence. He must be wise enough to debate with God. He must have a clear sense of justice to discern good from evil. At the same time, this person must be able to identify with what Job was going through, to have fellow feeling for his suffering, his struggle with doubt, his frustration at not being listened to, his weariness. Without these, he could never fathom the strength of Job's passion.

There are examples of mediation in the Old Testament. Abraham took this position when the Lord came to warn him that Sodom would be destroyed, and Abraham's nephew Lot was in danger with the rest of the city (Genesis 18:22–33). The Israelites persuaded Moses to act as go-between with God rather than face him themselves (Deuteronomy 5:5). Jeremiah reminded his contemporaries that the prophet's function included representing God to them and vice versa (Jeremiah 7:25–26). Isaiah saw the role of the Suffering Servant as that of a mediator (Isaiah 49:6; 53:4). It was a role that would involve sacrifice.

What Abraham and Moses fulfilled, what Isaiah predicted and what Job longed for has become a reality:

> For there is one God and one mediator between God and mankind, the man Christ Jesus.
> 1 TIMOTHY 2:5

This mediator satisfies the requirements more than we could have thought possible!

> Since we have a great high priest who has ascended into heaven, Jesus the Son of God, let us hold firmly to the faith we profess. For we do not have a high priest who is unable to feel sympathy for our weaknesses, but we have one who has been tempted in every way, just as we are – yet he did not sin.
> HEBREWS 4:14–15

> Such a high priest truly meets our need – one who is holy,
> blameless, pure, set apart from sinners, exalted above the
> heavens.
> HEBREWS 7:26

Jesus is exactly the mediator we need because he is not only able to
enter into our experiences but he is also able to bring those realities
into the very presence of God the Father.

> Christ Jesus who died – more than that, who was raised to life –
> is at the right hand of God and is also interceding for us.
> ROMANS 8:34

Job's tearful struggle need not be ours, unless we choose to ignore
the privileged access God has made possible to all who believe in
Jesus. There is someone able and willing to speak for us in heaven
itself!

Comment box: Redeemer – redemption

> I know that my redeemer lives, and that in the end he will
> stand upon the earth.
> JOB 19:25

This is probably the best-known verse in the book of Job, thanks
not least to Handel and his famous aria in 'Messiah'. It is also
used as the opening line to a hymn by Samuel Medley (1738–99):

I know that my Redeemer lives!
what comfort this sweet sentence gives!

However, the concept of redemption and the role of the
redeemer, once common in the ancient world and integral to the
life and worship of the Israelites, has largely fallen into disuse
except as a technical term in certain businesses. The banking
industry uses the term where a financial obligation, for example

a mortgage, is paid off with a lump sum. The core concept is that of 'buy back', where an object or person is 'redeemed' by the payment of an appropriate price.

Under Mosaic law, there were particularly strict regulations concerning property ownership. Following the settlement of the Israelites in the promised land, each family was allocated land which was to remain theirs in perpetuity. It might be sold to alleviate poverty but the right to buy it back either by the one who sold it or, on their death, by an appropriate relative known as the redeemer remained. There are examples of the practice in the Old Testament: see Ruth 4 and Jeremiah 32.

The other expression of redemption in the Old Testament, and one which is carried over into the New Testament, is that of release from slavery. It has its roots in the deliverance of Israel from slavery in Egypt.

> Then the Lord said to Moses... 'Say to the Israelites, "I am the Lord, and I will bring you out from under the yoke of the Egyptians. I will free you from being slaves to them and I will redeem you with an outstretched arm and with mighty acts of judgement."'
>
> EXODUS 6:1, 6

Redemption could be gained only as sin was forgiven through atonement – one life given for another – which was the basis of the sacrificial system of the tabernacle and the temple.

The concept of slavery as a metaphor of the hold that sin has over our lives carries over into the New Testament. The Greek word *apolutrosis* occurs nine times in scripture, and always with the idea of a ransom or price paid, i.e. redemption by a redeemer (see Matthew 20:28; Mark 10:45). Jesus was blunt about this: 'Everyone who sins is a slave to sin' (John 8:34).

Peter observes that 'people are slaves to whatever has mastered them' (2 Peter 2:19) – which is why we need a redeemer: we need to be redeemed from sin. As in the Old Testament, so in the New, for there to be redemption there must be a price paid.

> For you know that it was not with perishable things such as silver or gold that you were redeemed from the empty way of life handed down to you from your ancestors, but with the precious blood of Christ, a lamb without blemish and defect.
> 1 PETER 1:18–19

Paul urges his readers to remember that they have been bought with a price (1 Corinthians 6:20; 7:23). And the letter to the Hebrews describes how we are freed from slavery to sin by the death of Christ (Hebrews 2:14–15).

How remarkable that Job anticipated the privileges we are given in Christ.

When Job has spoken there is silence, as if arguments have been exhausted. The friends have nothing to add, no new angle to pursue. Job's intransigence renders further discussion futile. Job seems energised by the discussion; his sense of injustice has been provoked but his opponents have left the ring. A silent pause, a stalemate even.

For you to consider

- Is Job right to want to justify himself?

- Job was angry with God for being so elusive. Was he missing something?

- Job seems to make little allowance for the fact that his friends were willing to spend so much time trying to help him. Should he have made more effort to show his appreciation?

- How can the fact that Jesus is our mediator help us in encouraging those who suffer?

5

Interlude: chapter 28

Where can wisdom be found?
JOB 28:12

Start here: read chapter 28
- Not in mining for gold and precious gems
- Not in the market place of precious things
- God knows where wisdom is found

The search for wisdom

The lights dimmed in the auditorium; the members of the rock band put down their instruments and left the stage leaving the audience cheering, whistling and dancing. Unnoticed, a neatly dressed man slipped on to the stage and sat at the grand piano. As he put his hands to the keys a single spotlight snapped on, focusing its glare on him. The strains of Beethoven's 'Moonlight Sonata' began to drift across the crowd. At first, they barely noticed and then seemed surprised, mystified. Gradually, the crowd stilled and listened with rapt attention. The change of mood was total and captivating.

The exhausting debate of the last 25 chapters is at an end. It has offered, often in beautiful poetry, the turbulent exchange between Job and his friends, but with no real insight into the problem Job faces, no satisfactory answer to his questioning or his tears. But when we step into chapter 28, we feel that we hear a different music. The change of mood is instant and complete:

There is a mine for silver
  and a place where gold is refined.
JOB 28:1

This is a melody we haven't heard before, another voice, a fresh way of speaking. Gone is the defiant tone; even the question is changed. After more than 20 chapters of asking and answering, 'Why?', now the question is, 'Where?' It is still a search but now we know what we are looking for: wisdom.

A different voice, clearly, but whose is it? The almost serene tone of this chapter is in complete contrast to the increasingly tetchy three friends of Job. And although the punctuation might suggest otherwise, the speaker does not seem to be Job – not the Job of chapter 27 which precedes it, nor of chapter 29 which follows. Scholars and commentators suggest that this is the storyteller himself introducing an interlude providing a change of pace and, crucially, pointing us away from an obsession with the past to prepare us for other possibilities. Can we really hope to answer the problem of suffering by changing the question so profoundly? Yes, we can and we must.

In order to make progress in understanding our place in God's purposes, we need wisdom. 'Where can wisdom be found?' is the question posed in verse 12 and in verse 20. It acts as a refrain dividing the chapter into three parts: verses 1–11, 13–19 and 21–28.

The vivid imagery of chapter 28 would have been instantly recognisable to readers in ancient times but is far less so in ours. So let us first decipher the word-picture painted for us. From the opening sentence, we know that this is going to be about something of timeless value: silver and gold. This is followed by mention of iron and copper, valued for their usefulness rather than their beauty, and then of sapphires and gold nuggets. What the writer describes is the lengths to which men go to find them. Verses 1–11 describe ancient mining techniques.

I once saw a TV programme on honey gatherers in Asia, where a group of tribesmen cooperated to find honey down potholes or on the face of steep cliffs. Suspended on ropes of vines, men were lowered to find swarms with ripe honeycombs. One would smoke the bees with his flaming torch while the other cut off huge lumps of honeycomb with his machete, dropping them into a bag on his back. It is a similar picture described for us here, a sort of pot-holing with purpose. Men are lowered downs shafts to 'dangle and sway' as they search for precious gems and ore in the rock-face. Below the surface where food is grown, the darkness is 'transformed below as by fire' by the flaming torches they carry and jewels embedded in rock, glinting in their light. 'People assault the flinty rock with their hands' to harvest its treasure. Or, where there are no shafts, they 'tunnel through the rock' with the same determination; in places 'far from human dwellings' and where wild animals and birds cannot go, they 'bring hidden things to light'. But there is one thing more precious still that they do not find there: wisdom. So part one of the chapter closes with a challenge to part two:

> But where can wisdom be found?
> Where does understanding dwell?
> JOB 28:12

The deep places of the earth or the depths of the sea, for all their wonder and mystery, must admit, 'It is not in me.'

'Commodification' is the ugly word some use to describe the way society attempts to turn everything into something that can be bought or sold. 'Everything has its price,' they say. 'Consumerism rules OK.' Shopping has become a therapy! Having is not only desirable but a supreme good – even as we know that it isn't, we behave as if it were. The Bible tarnishes our stuff by reminding us that 'moths and vermin destroy and… thieves break in and steal' (Matthew 6:19). And no matter how rich we may become, we cannot buy health or intelligence. Nor, this chapter reminds us, can we buy wisdom, though we offer 'the finest of gold' or weighty silver, or precious onyx.

There is an important point made here which we may miss because it is so out of tune with modern values: wisdom is supremely valuable. The Bible regards it as something we need above everything else.

> The beginning of wisdom is this: get wisdom.
>   Though it cost you all you have, get understanding.
> PROVERBS 4:7

Maybe we need to consider what wisdom is and why it is so important.

The character of wisdom

Wisdom is not the same as knowledge. Being clever is not the same as being wise, just as being intellectual is not to be confused with being intelligent. If it were a matter of knowledge, ours would be the wisest society in the history of humankind! With a few clicks on my smartphone, an incalculable range of information is available to me from libraries and museums around the world. I can dip into the personal correspondence of Henry VIII, or find an explanation of the nature of black holes, or discover the performance of a cardiologist in my local hospital, or a recipe for this evening's dinner. The internet has opened up to us a seemingly infinite wealth of knowledge. But, even if we had the time, the inclination and the sheer brainpower for exhaustive study, we might still not be wise because wisdom is not found merely in the accumulation of knowledge.

Wisdom and knowledge are different from one another as an encyclopaedia is different from a dictionary; the one offers description, the other definition. Knowledge is about facts and wisdom is about meaning, broadly speaking. Knowledge tells us what a thing is; wisdom tells us what to do with it. Imagine a shovel: knowledge will describe its size and shape, and even its purpose; wisdom will tell us to use it to clear the snow from the path. Knowledge will retell the parables of Jesus; wisdom will enable us to understand what they mean. According to the *Cambridge English Dictionary* wisdom is 'the ability to use your knowledge and experience to make good decisions and judgements'.

This chapter in Job, then, should make us pause for thought, as it takes us in a different direction from our contemporary culture and perhaps even requires us to think differently about our faith. It offers an alternative point of reference for the way we live. Let's try to apply this view of wisdom to one profound issue which dominates Job's anxiety: what is my life all about; why are these things happening; what does it all mean? We find ourselves in the company of unnumbered others who ask the same question. I tried doing an online search for 'What is the meaning of life?' In 0.64 seconds, it offered me 201,000,000 results (yes, 201 million!).

This is not a new concern, nor is it limited to a handful of insecure individuals. You might have expected that science and technology had solved the riddle long ago; after all, they are uncovering more and more about our universe, our world and ourselves than ever before. But it is not enough to know how the solar system is sustained with such precision, how our thumbs can be so dexterous, what makes our mobile phones work. We need to know more than the what and the how; we want to know why. Why is there something rather than nothing? Where do I fit in the grand scheme of things? These are questions no algorithm can answer. Nor is it merely a matter of greater investment. Lack of wisdom and lack of resources are not necessarily connected. Being clever and rich is not the answer. This is what Job 28 is telling us.

By now, we are getting the impression that wisdom is to be highly valued, more so than a PhD in microbiology or an expedition to the rainforest or an investment in the most profitable of companies. We will not find it listed on eBay or Amazon, though doubtless they will offer some of the tens of thousands of books written about wisdom. 'The price of wisdom is beyond rubies' (28:18), so, 'Where can wisdom be found?' (28:12).

God understands the way to it
  and he alone knows where it dwells.
JOB 28:23

God has made everything and God sees everything. He is willing to share his insights with us so that we are able to use our knowledge and experience to make good decisions and judgements that will bring fulfilment and meaning to our lives. It may not be what we expect or even what we at first would prefer. It will almost certainly run counter to the intellectual and social ethos of our times. In fact, it may even challenge our own spirituality and the culture of our church family. But there is no doubting the way to wisdom; it is stated so clearly – and surprisingly – right here:

[God] said to the human race,
  'The fear of the Lord – that is wisdom,
  and to shun evil is understanding.'
JOB 28:28

That needs some unpacking!

The fear of the Lord

'What comes into our minds when we think about God is the most important thing about us.'[10] Really? Yes, really. Our view of God determines pretty much everything else. It will profoundly affect how we see ourselves, how we relate to one another, our moral standards, how we view our future, our response to those who are vulnerable, even how we spend our money! Consciously or otherwise, this is foundational to who we are.

Of course, this is not a commonly held view today. God has been largely excluded from the modern mindset. It is assumed that we live in a closed universe, that there is no one 'out there' breaking in to impose his will or purpose on us, certainly no creator or designer.

Darwinian evolution is the matrix governing far more than biology, the lens through which almost every topic is viewed or considered. In the realm of morals, society has evolved from the Dark Age of 'right' and 'wrong' to be accepting of acts and attitudes that would have scandalised previous generations. As part of this progressive society, even we who are Christians blink at the suggestion that 'the fear of God' is good and desirable. It seems so 'Old Testament'! Our children sing heartily and happily, 'Our God is a great big God,' as if he were brother to Roald Dahl's Big Friendly Giant. The God we talk and sing about is warm and friendly, cuddly even. And, anyway, doesn't Jesus call us to love God and isn't it John who tells us that there 'is no fear in love'? Maybe this concept of fearing God has outlived its use-by date! Or are we missing something important?

What is this 'fear of God' that is mentioned quite often, particularly in the Old Testament, but not exclusively so? Clearly, this is not the same as being frightened or scared. Time and again, the Bible encourages us not to be afraid. This is not the sort of fear a person suffers as the result of a fear of heights or spiders. This fear is a profound response to something or someone so distinct and different from us, so much more than we are, that we are in awe of him. This is reverence, the response commonly reported in scripture when a human being is confronted with the presence of God or one of his angels: they fall down before them. Sadly, our common word 'awe' has been largely evacuated of meaning by the use of 'awesome' to describe a meal or an advert or a new dress – or even a radio programme. We need to rescue and recycle the word because we have no substitutes to express a sense of wonder which rises above the trivial. When used of God, this fear is more about wonder than terror, love than anger, amazement than horror, respect than humiliation.

Here, as elsewhere in the Bible, 'the fear of God' is viewed as very important and highly desirable. Indeed, you could say it is considered as fundamental in those who believe in God. My generation was taught in Sunday School to memorise Bible verses and one of the first I recall was this:

The fear of the Lord is the beginning of wisdom,
  the knowledge of the Holy One is understanding.
PROVERBS 9:10

The same idea is found repeatedly through Psalms (e.g. 111:10) and in Proverbs (e.g. 1:7; 3:7; 15:33). Notice that this fear of God is not the goal but the means towards the goal, which is wisdom. True wisdom is not achievable without it. If this is so, the implications are serious for us. If the notion of fearing God is so remote from contemporary Christian experience and if this fear is, as it were, the first step along the road to true spiritual wisdom, what does that say about the degree of wisdom we have attained? Presumably, that we need to do some serious thinking.

So what is the connection between the fear of God and wisdom? How does the one lead to the other? Abraham was a great man of faith but that faith sprang from his fear (Genesis 22:12). He was in awe of God's greatness and power to the extent that he could even be willing to risk the death of his only son. Surely, that is true wisdom!

Isaiah has much to say about the coming Messiah:

The Spirit of the Lord will rest on him –
  the Spirit of wisdom and of understanding,
  the Spirit of counsel and of might,
  the Spirit of the knowledge and fear of the Lord –
and he will delight in the fear of the Lord.
ISAIAH 11:2–3

Dreadful as the prospect of the cross was for Jesus, it was possible because of his unshakeable confidence in his Father. His delight in the fear of the Lord took him to the ultimate sacrifice. And the fear of the Lord became a distinguishing characteristic of the early church too: '[the church] enjoyed a time of peace and was strengthened. Living in the fear of the Lord and encouraged by the Holy Spirit, it increased in numbers' (Acts 9:31).

What we believe about God is crucial. 'It is impossible to keep our moral practices sound and our inward attitudes right while our idea of God is erroneous or inadequate.'[11] The focus of the book of Job has been on Job up to this point. Was he really such a good man? Has he deserved the terrible things that have happened to him and his family? What does he need to do about it? In chapter 28, the narrator points us in a different direction, not to the answer but in the direction in which the answer is more likely to be found:

> God understands the way to it [wisdom]
>   and he alone knows where it dwells…
> And he said to the human race,
>   'The fear of the Lord – that is wisdom.'
> JOB 28:23, 28

For you to consider

- Think about an experience you may have had of an overpowering sense of the greatness or holiness of God. How would you describe the impact it has made on you since?

- What do you find most challenging/disturbing about the idea of fearing God?

- How are we to balance the fear of God with the knowledge that God is a loving Father?

- What would you say to someone who thinks that Christians use God as a crutch?

Part II

There is another way:
chapters 29—37

6

Job's last word: chapters 29—31

How I long for the months gone by,
    for the days when God watched over me,
when his lamp shone on my head
    and by his light I walked through darkness!
JOB 29:2–3

The interlude ended, we, the readers, return to the rubbish dump, but with a fresh perspective and the encouragement to take a larger view. Job and his friends – we are soon to discover there is a fourth – have not shared in the interlude but they too seem to have reached a different place. Job has grown more confident in the things he believes about God. He seems to have reflected on the discussion so far and now knows what he must say in response. One writer describes this final speech as 'Job's last stand'.[12]

I cannot imagine these strong chapters being spoken while Job sits meekly on a pile of refuse. I see him striding up and down, declaiming, pointing and gesticulating to add force and conviction to his words. He has come a long way from the pathetic whimpers of his lamentation (chapter 3). He is clear now that the accusations of his friends are empty but the haunting questions remain, waiting an explanation. What is all this about? Why has this happened to me, of all people? And these stir deeper, older questions – What does life itself mean? – asked since the gates of Eden shut against the human race.

Human beings are the only creatures who ask questions or feel the need to do so. (Imagine your budgie asking you about the meaning of life!)

A great many people in the West today… believe that life is
an accidental evolutionary phenomenon which has no more
intrinsic meaning than a fluctuation of the breeze or a rumble
in the gut.

Terry Eagleton[13]

The influence of secular scientific thinking challenges the innate
idea that we are somehow significant and significantly different from
the animal kingdom. But why are we different? Why are we here at
all? Philosophers like Eagleton are ready to discuss and write about
the matter but, infuriatingly, they are obsessed with analysing the
question rather than answering it. He does, however, observe:

Perhaps it is impossible to generalise intelligently about human
life, because in order to do so we would have to step outside
it… Surely someone outside human existence altogether, like
God, would be able to survey it as a whole and see whether it
added up?[14]

Unlike Eagleton, Job has certainly grasped the point. The answers
to these questions are not found in some abstract world where
there is only God and ourselves. They must be explained within the
web of our daily lives, with the diversity and complexity of all our
relationships – family, community and nation, the vast network of
interlocking people, institutions and fellowships (religious and non-
religious). What happens to them affects us and, surprisingly, vice
versa. If Job – and we – are to progress towards understanding,
we must do so in the real context in which we find ourselves. This
requires clear-eyed honesty, which is precisely what we find in Job's
last speech. By the time he concludes, we will know precisely how
he sees his life in the past and the present, and how he intends to
face the future.

Know where you have been: chapter 29

Start here: read chapter 29

- Job longs for the time when God was near
- Job recalls when he was respected
- Job remembers his advice being sought

Job's present contrasts sharply with the past that he recalls in this chapter. Things used to be so different. Before the disasters that befell him, he was held in high esteem within the community. We touch another culture here, one that is unfamiliar to us in the postmodern West. In the ancient Middle East, morality was largely determined in terms of honour and shame rather than innocence and guilt. The issue was not so much whether one's behaviour complied with certain laws but what its impact was on the community. Human beings are social creatures and have to find ways to live together that are mutually beneficial. It is sensible, therefore, for them to agree together that certain behaviours are acceptable to the community and others are not. Those whose behaviour takes account of the wider group will be honoured by their peers and those who act against the best interests of the community will be shamed (see below).

Comment: Honour-shame or innocence-guilt?

Far from being honoured, Job was mocked, laughed at and humiliated by people who themselves lived shamefully. Even the street urchins made his life a misery. We have no problem feeling for Job in this, but we may also feel that he makes a great deal of fuss about it. Certainly, to our Western culture, this would not feature as a 'first-order' issue as it seems to be for Job, and that is because our presuppositions are significantly different. We tend to overlook a feature of biblical revelation which is to be found from Genesis to Revelation which recognises the importance of honour and shame in God's relationship with humanity.

I first stumbled on the honour-shame basis for morality in the story of a convert from Islam. Nabeel Qureshi explains that the authority structure among Muslims is based on the relationship with those who are respected by the community. Their word provides the moral framework and, out of respect for them, it is above questioning by group members. How well a person meets those social expectations determines a person's virtue, not their personal beliefs about right and wrong.[15]

In the West, authority is determined by reason and is thus open to question by individuals as to what is right and wrong. In Islamic cultures, shame rather than guilt is critical and is given higher consideration than laws or moral codes. Hence, in extreme examples, a person's honour may be avenged by murder and violence.

The honour-shame paradigm of morality is, however, far more widespread than Islam. It is a dominant influence in Chinese and Japanese cultures where 'loss of face' is feared. And it is also very much in evidence in scripture, particularly in God's promise to keep his people from shame and his promise to honour those who honour him. Although honour-shame and innocence-guilt appear to be mutually exclusive, that is not how the Bible regards them, for it appeals to both. David writes in the Psalms:

My salvation and my honour depend on God.
PSALM 62:7

Blot out my transgressions. Wash away all my iniquity and cleanse me from my sin.
PSALM 51:2

The first verse relates to honour-shame and the second to innocence-guilt.

Similarly, Isaiah writes about forgiveness for guilt in one chapter and shame in the next:

He was pierced for our transgressions.
ISAIAH 53:5

Do not be afraid for you will not suffer shame.
ISAIAH 54:4

Paul, too, writes about 'falling short of the glory of God' (shame) and about being 'justified freely by grace' (from guilt) – and that in the same sentence (Romans 3:23–24). Guilt and shame, innocence and honour are never far apart in the work of the inspired writers since they represent two sides of the same coin. The great events of the Bible's story reflect this same reality. We see the Israelites delivered from the shame of slavery in due course to become the leading nation of the region under the kingship of David. Supremely, of course, we see the two blended into one in the gospel, and never more clearly than in Paul's statement concerning Jesus:

Who, being in very nature God,
   did not consider equality with God something to be used
to his own advantage;
   rather, he made himself nothing,
   by taking the very nature of a servant,
   being made in human likeness.
And being found in appearance as a man,

> he humbled himself
>   by becoming obedient to death – even death on a cross!
> Therefore, God exalted him to the highest place
>   and gave him a name that is above every name.
> PHILIPPIANS 2:6–9
>
> Whether we feel our need because of shame or guilt, whether we seek honour or forgiveness, the way to the restoration of our dignity and justification before God is the same – through faith in Jesus. And through him the way is opened into the presence of God and ultimately the joy and glory of heaven.

In the past, Job had shown himself an upstanding member of his community. He was a generous philanthropist, responding to the poor and providing for orphans (29:12), relieving the anxiety of a dying man by taking responsibility for his widow (29:13), supporting the blind man and running errands for those with physical disabilities (29:15), and standing up for those who needed an advocate (29:16–17). The extent of his kindness and compassion was known and honoured across town. When he walked the streets and sat in the public square, people showed him due respect. As a natural leader in the community, his advice was sought and taken (29:21–25).

Job had assumed that his life would continue in much the same way until old age brought him to the end of his days within his own home and among his loved ones. No wonder that he found his present situation so perplexing – and painful. Maybe it would have been better to have forgotten the past, to have walked away, accepting that life is never as secure as we assume. Nostalgia is not always helpful!

For reflection: Job 29:2–4

How I long for the days gone by,
  for the days when God watched over me,

> when his lamp shone on my head
>   and by his light I walked through darkness!
> Oh for the days when I was in my prime,
>   when God's intimate friendship blessed my house.
>
> JOB 29:2–4

What pathos, what longing, what loss! Job looked back on a relationship which now was only a memory. He had lost his prime and he had lost his children: he might have expected the first but not the second. But the loss he feels still more is the loss of the close friendship of God. Let us pause here for a moment. We associate knowing God personally with the New Testament rather than the Old, but here it is spoken of in the richest terms: 'God watched over me'; 'his lamp shone on my head'; and 'God's intimate friendship blessed my house'. This was not vague religious emotion or sentiment. nor was it a formal ritual association. Job speaks of God as a close friend, someone he knew personally and who knew him in return. John wrote of this: 'We know that we have come to know him' (1 John 2:3). From Job to Jesus to John, the same reality is announced: we human beings may know God and know him personally. Indeed, it is what we were made to enjoy when God created us in his likeness and walked with our first parents, Adam and Eve, 'in the cool of the day' (Genesis 3:8).

But it is not always like this: just as there is the possibility for ordinary human beings like Job – and you and me – to know God, so there is the reality that sometimes God seems at a distance from us. 'The dark night of the soul' is, sadly, possible even for people of outstanding spirituality. Indeed, many of the most notable people in the Bible experienced what one might describe as spiritual depression. Moses, David, Elijah, Jeremiah – all of them felt abandoned at some point in their lives. Indeed, David wrote songs about this and Jeremiah a whole book! John the Baptist, too, though he had been 'filled with the Holy Spirit even before he [was] born' (Luke 1:15) and had heard God affirm Jesus as his Son, experienced the darkness of doubt as to whether Jesus was the Messiah. William Cowper (1731–1800), friend of John Newton, wrote a hymn which may sound quaint to some but expresses the same theme well:

Where is the blessedness I knew
when first I saw the Lord?
Where is that soul-refreshing view
of Jesus and his word?

What peaceful hours I once enjoyed!
How sweet their memory still!
But they have left an aching void
the world can never fill.

Why should this be? There are no pat answers. From person to person, from one time to another, the explanation will vary, but the fact that it happens is not what it seems, as Job was soon to discover. God might have withdrawn himself for a time, but he had not abandoned his servant. Nor does he abandon us.

As a boy, I was puzzled by a hymn we sang occasionally. It had lines which I remember as:

Here I raise my Ebenezers,
hither by Thine help I'm come.

What, I wondered, are Ebenezers? Eventually, I discovered that this was a reference to a Bible story found in 1 Samuel 7 and to a memorial erected by Samuel to remind the people that God had delivered them from their perennial enemy, the Philistines. The poetic intention of the hymn writer was to encourage Christians to remember God's blessings in the past and draw strength from them for the present. Sadly, Job missed the opportunity to do the same as he called to mind his past experience of community life. Paul writes about the danger of being locked in the past, of relying on it rather than pressing forward (see Philippians 3). But there is a way of using the past to inspire and strengthen us in the present and for the future. By calling to mind the good that we have experienced, we will remind ourselves what God has done in our lives, remembering our real achievements, not so as to promote ourselves but to recall what is possible for us. This honest assessment will better equip us to cope with the future.

> I say to everyone of you: do not think of yourself more highly than you ought, but rather think of yourself with sober judgement.
> ROMANS 12:3

Our sport-obsessed, competitive culture is interested only in winners. You may not be one of them, but that doesn't mean you are nothing! Think about those people you have been able to help, those you have encouraged, those acts of kindness that seemed to go unnoticed by others (but not by God), that card you posted, that call you made, that coin you dropped into the hat on the pavement, that New Testament you gave away, that check-out operator you spoke gently to after the ill-tempered customer they had just served, that person whom you entrusted with new responsibilities – and so on. Every evidence of the fruit of the Spirit in your life was noticed by God; be sure you don't forget it yourself!

Rather than only looking back with regret as Job did, remember with gratitude. Draw on the past to cope with the problems of the present and to face the challenges of the future.

Know where you are: chapter 30

Start here: read chapter 30
- The character of Job's mockers
- Assaults and suffering
- God's apparent silence

The past for Job is the polar opposite of the present. If he was honoured then, he is shamed now. With hard-edged realism, he reflects on the situation in which he finds himself and burns at the injustice of it all. There is a form of spirituality that requires us always to be cheerful, optimistic and full of faith. Anything less might lead to questions about our standing as Christians. 'Victorious Christian living', it's sometimes called – but it is phoney and unbiblical.

Just as the Bible is honest about the failings of its 'heroes', so it reveals the doubts and fears that they carried on their walk of faith. Moses 'lost it' several times when faced with seemingly impossible situations. David struggled when he saw enemies prosper at his expense, and stumbled when he lusted after a neighbour. Peter's closeness to Jesus did not prevent his denials. So we should not feel shocked when plain-speaking Job expresses his sense of injustice.

Job's humiliations

In every society, there are those about whom it is difficult to speak without either being politically incorrect or seeming snobbish! How are we to refer to those who are antisocial, who make themselves objectionable, who are selfish criminals, who take delight in breaching social conventions, who are shameless and deliberately hostile? Job struggles to describe them too in the opening verses of chapter 30. His opinion of them is so low he wouldn't even entrust his dog to them! Refusing to work, they live as scavengers on the fringes of society. You sense Job's disgust that even their children mock him, that they make up silly songs to taunt him. They play practical jokes on him, spitting in this face. Things are so bad Job is terrified of running into a group of them or of having them jump out on him. It was unbearably humiliating.

'Oh,' say some, 'pride comes before a fall!' (see Proverbs 16:18). We wouldn't feel humiliated if we were humble. But humility is a much-misunderstood virtue, not a bit like the toadying attitude of Uriah Heap in Dickens' *David Copperfield*. It is about being who we are – nothing more, nothing less. It is not humility for the professional dancer to claim that she cannot dance properly, or for the craftsman to deny his skill, or for the rich person to suggest that he is poor. It's about that 'sober judgement' to which Paul refers (Romans 12:3), about being realistic about our strengths and weaknesses. We cease to be humble when we slide into making comparisons, seeing ourselves as better than others. It was not pride that made the mockery of the riff-raff so painful to Job; it was the implication that he was not an upright man, that he was being punished for his sins. What could be worse than to be condemned by those who so obviously deserved to be shamed?

Job's expectations

Religion, some say, is for those who can't cope with the rigours of life. I can't speak for other faiths but this is certainly not the case so far as Christianity is concerned. The person who turns to Christ in the hope of finding an easier path through life's problems discovers that Jesus offers them a cross to carry, a narrow way to walk and warnings that his followers can expect to be treated in much the same way as he was. Yet, in spite of the clear evidence to the contrary, we still expect that good things will invariably happen to good people and bad things will happen only to bad people.

Far from guaranteeing an easy life, faith in Christ adds another dimension. By bringing God into the picture, we have to grapple with questions as to why he permits things to happen which seem to contradict his love and care. The atheist ought to have an easier time of it. His world is subject to random forces for which there is no explanation, other than 'Things happen!' If he gives in to traditional ways of thinking and asks, 'Why?' the only answer possible is, 'Why not?' Only when one admits a loving God does 'the question of evil' become a question at all.

Job's reasonable expectation was that, as he had been faithful to God in his family, in his business, in society and in his personal life, God would show his faithfulness by blessing him. Instead, he feels betrayed:

> God has unstrung my bow and afflicted me.
> JOB 30:11

> I cry out to you, God, but you do not answer;
>   I stand up, but you merely look at me.
> You turn on me ruthlessly.
> JOB 30:20–21

This is no way for God to treat someone who has been faithful, surely. But, as Job has already said to his friends, the only explanation he can see is that God is responsible for what has happened to him.

> Ask the animals, and they will teach you,
>   or the birds of the air and they will tell you…
>   or let the fish in the sea inform you.
> Which of all these does not know
>   that the hand of the Lord has done this?
> JOB 12:7–9

When faced with a dilemma, the natural response of those who know God is to pray, as Job had done. Sadly, this served to add to his problems rather than solve them. In fact, it seemed to Job as if God had used it as an opportunity to turn on him 'ruthlessly' and attack him (30:21). 'Prayer moves the hand that moves the world,' they say, but it didn't seem to work for Job.

I wonder how many tens of thousands of books about prayer have been written. Over the years, I have probably read dozens, seeking to understand better how prayer works and why sometimes it doesn't. There is no doubt that prayer is important; we have the example and the teaching of Jesus to that effect. We have the example of the early church in Acts and the New Testament letters. We have the rich record of Christian history and the devotional richness of our hymnody. We know that, as one hymn writer puts it, 'Prayer is the Christian's vital breath'. And we have the experience of God answering our prayers – sometimes. But the pain kicks in when heaven seems to have grown deaf to our cries.

> Yet when I hoped for good, evil came;
>   when I looked for light, then came darkness.
> The churning inside me never stops;
>   days of suffering confront me.
> JOB 30:26–27

Job's religion was not a crutch: it was a challenge.

> My skin grows black and peels;
>   my body burns with fever.
> JOB 30:30

It is a living death, so 'my lyre is tuned to mourning' (30:31). We are at the centre of Job's anguish still and there is more to come. As yet, there is no light at the end of the tunnel. Perhaps that is where we are personally, too. God seems so far away; heaven seems shut up against us; we too hoped for good and instead evil turned up (30:26). And there is tomorrow, and tomorrow, and tomorrow. But Job is not about to give up; nor shall we. He has a strategy for that tomorrow.

Know where you are going: chapter 31

Start here: read chapter 31
- Job commits to holiness
- Job commits to justice and generosity
- Job longs to put his case to God personally

It is obvious that dwelling on the past is not going to resolve Job's present difficulties. He is still suffering physically and spiritually as he feels deeply the injustice of what he is going through. His sense of alienation from God distresses him above all else.

If only Job could explain things from his own perspective and demonstrate his innocence of the wrongs for which, he assumes, he is being punished. So, he sets out his determination to appear at the bar of God's justice to plead his cause – a determination that will require him to demonstrate moral and spiritual integrity.

Job creates the atmosphere of a courtroom by making his appeal as a series of 'oaths of clearance'. This was a legal device, a negative confession. 'A crime could be disowned by calling down a curse on oneself if one had committed it.'[16] The more usual form of defence would be to challenge the accuser to produce evidence of wrongdoing. Job's friends had accused him of a variety of sins but they had offered nothing more than their 'no smoke without fire' assumption by way of proof. Job now uses a series of oaths to clear his name along the lines of 'If I have done A, then let my punishment be B'. This is not an appeal to his peers but to God, for it is his standing before God that is Job's concern above everything else.

Job was not a lawyer so his case is not divided into neat categories, delivered with dispassionate objectivity. At times, the sin and the punishment are balanced; at times, one or other is missing. This is spoken with all the passion of offended dignity and strident integrity. But Job, weakened by grief, by deep physical suffering and the burning heat of the unshadowed rubbish dump, knows that everything he is as a human being, a husband, a believer in God is at stake.

As we listen, we realise that he is using the past to shape his future path. 'This is the person I have been and this is the person I will continue to be.' If I have been dishonest, then may others profit from it rather than me (31:7–8). If I have committed adultery – even in my mind – then may my wife repay me with unfaithfulness (31:9–10). If I have threatened the vulnerable with violence or used my influence against those who have none, 'let my arm fall from the shoulder' so that I am stripped of power (31:21–22). While there are echoes of the ten commandments here, there is also anticipation of the sermon on the mount. Job is prepared to be tested in matters that are personal rather than social, private rather than public. He pinpoints lust, falsehood, desire, greed, selfishness, covetousness, idolatry, gloating, swearing and lack of compassion.

It is one thing for Job to say that he will do no wrong, but he goes further: he is prepared to put the welfare of others on the line by his oath-making. As God watches his every step, Job says, 'So will I!' He will be careful what and whom he looks at – and how. Beware the pretty girls (31:1); Job will be careful not to loiter (31:9); Job will be meticulously honest in his dealings (31:6); Job will keep his heart open to those in need (31:16–22); Job will not waste time on miserly asset-counting (31:24–28); Job will be sensitive to the suffering of others (31:29). He will even be concerned for the environment (31:38). In short, Job will in future order his life to avoid unnecessary exposure to temptation.

Job is motivated in all this by fear: not fear of other people, whether individuals or 'clans' (31:33–34). It is God that he fears:

I dreaded destruction from God,
 and for fear of his splendour I could not do such things.
JOB 31:23

Job had issued a challenge to God – but how would God respond? Anything would be better than heaven's silence (31:35). If only God would say something, or write an indictment against Job setting out his sins and offences – even that would be better than nothing. He would wear such a document with dignity, displaying it so that all could see that what was happening to him was just, that he deserved the disasters that had befallen him and his family. Then Job could attempt to respond to the accusation point by point, to engage with God and plead for mercy where he had done wrong (31:37).

Notice how the chapter concludes: 'The words of Job are ended.' Job sinks to the ground, exhausted by this last vehement declaration. There is nothing more he can say. A ripple passes through the listening friends, not of sympathy but of anger that Job still refuses to face the obvious. They are not impressed by his oaths or his passion. Their frustration at being unable to convince him of his wrong remains, stronger than ever (32:1–3).

We have not yet reached the point of resolution for Job, but already we can learn from the way in which he faces the harsh reality of his circumstances. This can help us in our response to the challenges we face. The first and most obvious lesson is the need to be realistic, no matter how much we long for change. It is not holiness or piety to behave as if our circumstances did not exist or that they were other than they are, or to pretend that we are utterly immune to them. Until we honestly face our circumstances, we cannot begin to deal with the consequences. We will not seek the grace we need, the support that is available, the strength to begin to cope with things as they are.

Out present is not without a past. There is value in looking back, beyond the beginnings of the pain and the gathering of the clouds. Every experience of God's grace and love, or our friends' support, of effectiveness and self-confidence – these may be 'the past' but they have a message for us for today as well. The God who blessed us then is still the same God. The achievements of the past are achievements still, written in the rocks of history and the records of heaven. We may not have medals or rosettes or honours or degrees with which to decorate our walls, but the memory of having done well, of receiving the respect of others, is still relevant. There is refreshment to draw from the well of our own story. Job's mistake was to look back with sad nostalgia; it didn't have to be like that.

Job's determination to face the future, his resolution and courage are, however, deeply impressive. What an example he is to us! Gone is the whimpering self-pity; he is ready to challenge heaven itself as he faces tomorrow. Though he feared God, Job seemed to sense that God would not be offended by his anger and boldness. Far from it.

Some, when faced with unexpected difficulties, turn in desperation to God, but feel that God ignores them in their hour of need. They are disappointed that their prayers are not answered in the way they hoped and before long they give up – on prayer and on God. Their previous reputation as Christians is soon forgotten. It could have been me – or you, perhaps. What will keep us from following the same route to spiritual oblivion?

Faith! Perhaps expressed with the same force and conviction as Job's last speech, or perhaps with a weary whisper, but faith nonetheless. For Job knew that, for all that he suffered, what was true about God when Job was prosperous was true when Job was penniless. And even though he was soon to discover things about God which went far beyond his earlier understanding, he knew that God does not change. Similarly, for you and for me: God did not change the day you were made redundant, or were given a diagnosis of cancer, or learned of the tragic death of a friend (Malachi 3:6).

James also reminds us that our heavenly Father 'does not change like shifting shadows' (James 1:17). God is utterly dependable.

Job understands the implications of this: he will not only believe; he will behave! He will not use his disappointment to excuse lower standards, to give way to his weaknesses. The fact that his upright life has not resulted in unfettered happiness will not deter him from continuing to live to please God. Yes, he had hoped for better and he cannot understand why it has not been granted, but he will still be honest, though others doubt him; he will still be honourable, though ragamuffins taunt him. Though all that remains to him is his walk with God without its attendant joy, he will choose this pathway.

This is practical faith, to trust God even though reason and emotions protest, although the clouds envelop us. We know that beyond them the sun still shines. Job's patience was rewarded, as will ours be.

For you to consider

- How does Job's approach parallel your own experience? Does it cast any light on how you might respond to your present circumstances?

- Why not write your own testimony? Describe how you came to faith in Christ, what difference it made to you and how it could affect your future.

- Do you know someone who is having a difficult time? Is there anything you have learnt from Job that might be an encouragement to them?

- When there seems to be no hope, where can hope be found – and how?

7

Elihu's first and last word: chapters 32—37

Start here: read chapter 32
- The fourth friend is introduced
- Why he has been a silent participant so far
- Why he has now joined in the discussion

Job has exhausted his arguments and himself. His is an inner struggle between his strong sense of personal integrity and his equally strong belief in a just and holy God. There seems to be no way through or out of the impasse – when another friend steps forward and another voice is heard. Elihu has, it seems, been present all the time, listening and taking careful note of what was being said on both sides but until now he has kept a respectful silence. The time has come, he decides, for a fresh approach.

There are widely divergent views of Elihu's contribution. Some commentators see his speeches as an intrusion that is so out of touch that they must have been added later by another writer. Some regard him as a 'shallow pretender' or a 'vain conceited upstart' while another admires him as 'an exponent of reasonableness'. So what will we make of him? We will not always find him easy to understand or interpret, but we cannot dismiss his contribution. The fact that Elihu is given more uninterrupted space than anyone else in the book suggests that he has something to say that we, the readers, need to consider.

Elihu does not start well. Here is a young man who seems to be full of his own importance. Admittedly, he had shared the overwhelming sadness of Job's condition and had sat quietly through many days of frustrating debate in the stench and heat of the rubbish dump. He had listened to the older men debating with Job what had caused his sufferings and had been increasingly annoyed with them. At the same time, he was losing patience with Job's stubborn refusal to admit that he was more concerned with his own reputation than God's. The final straw was when the three friends had nothing to say by way of response to Job's last speech.

> Elihu... became very angry with Job for justifying himself rather than God. He was also angry with the three friends, because they found no way to refute Job, and yet had condemned him.
> JOB 32:2–3

The reason he had stayed quiet for so long was out of respect for his elders (32:7). But, having listened to the older men, it was, Elihu felt, his turn to say something. He even feels that he had an advantage over them in that he had not been the butt of Job's arguments (32:14). Eventually, he could stay silent no more.

> Inside I am like bottled-up wine,
>   like new wineskins ready to burst.
> I must speak and find relief,
>   I must open my lips and reply.
> JOB 32:19–20

Clearly, this was a different culture from our own! We begin to feel uncomfortable as Elihu sets out his own 'qualifications' as a contributor to the discussion, perhaps revealing more about his culture than his character (33:2–3, 5–7).

There are things to say in Elihu's favour. Although the three friends seemed to ignore anything that Job said, Elihu has listened carefully to him and takes the trouble to quote and then answer his concerns. And he repeatedly refers to Job by name. From the outset, Elihu makes clear to Job that he is on Job's side: 'I want you to be cleared'

(33:32). This sets a different tone from the finger-pointing speeches of the three friends.

Elihu makes four speeches. At the end of the first, chapters 32 and 33, he invites a response from Job. The second he addresses to the 'wise men', but they too make no response. At times, Elihu seems to ramble, apparently contradicting himself. He is certainly less than easy to follow. But he 'opens up the theme of wisdom, which is a theological bridge in the story between Job's experience and his hearing the Lord'.[17]

God is greater than we are: chapter 33

Start here: read chapter 33
- Job is invited to discuss with Elihu
- Explains God's apparent silence
- Suggests God's rescue plan
- Invites a response

Job, Elihu suggests, has a distorted view of what had been happening to him so he holds up a mirror to the situation as if to say, 'Do you realise what you are saying, Job?'

> You have said in my hearing –
>   I heard the very words –
> 'I am pure, I have done no wrong;
>   I am clean and free from sin.
> Yet God has found fault with me;
>   he considers me his enemy.'
> JOB 33:8–10

It was as if Job was saying that God was not only unfair but also unjust, ignoring his cries and punishing him for sins he had never committed: 'There is no profit in trying to please God' (34:9). Not so, says Elihu. We have to see the situation we are in as part of a bigger picture, as something consistent with bigger realities.

> Far be it from God to do evil,
>   from the Almighty to do wrong.
> He repays everyone for what they have done…

> It is unthinkable that God would do wrong,
>   that the Almighty would pervert justice.
> JOB 34:10–12

God is incapable of sin or injustice. 'Can someone who hates justice govern?' asks Elihu (34:17). It is unthinkable!

Underlying this assertion is the idea that some things are true and are always true. That does not sit easily with the idea that we each have our own truth, that none of us is wrong – or right, for that matter. Elihu is arguing for something else: that there are some things we can say about God that are true and are always true, no matter how others may want us to unsay them. God is always just, always compassionate, always holy. What he was to Job, he was to Abraham, Moses, Elijah, Daniel, Zechariah, Jonah, John the Baptist, Peter, Saul of Tarsus, Chrysostom, Bernard of Clairvaux, William Tyndale, William Wilberforce, Billy Graham – and you and me this very day. This is why the Bible is so relevant and faith can be so confident. We have to learn to live our lives within the framework of what is true, of eternal and spiritual realities. God *is* greater than we are.

Perhaps, then, Job has been missing something (33:14). Elihu suggests two possibilities: God speaks by direct revelation through dreams and visions (33:15) or suffering (33:19). In the days before the Bible was complete, dreams and visions seem to have been more common than today, though one hears of them still among those who do not have access to scripture. The other is more difficult to receive: it is not that God is using suffering as a punishment for sin; rather, it is that God may use it as a messenger.

> God whispers to us in our pleasures, speaks in our consciences, but shouts in our pain; it is his megaphone to rouse a deaf world.
> C.S. Lewis[18]

It is this readiness of God to speak that has given us the Bible. Over thousands of years, people speaking different languages, with different backgrounds and levels of education, were inspired to write in response to what the Spirit of God was saying to and through them. The result is not just a textbook for one religious group, or the history of one race, or a handbook of spiritual philosophy, or a theological masterpiece; it is God's letter to the human race, the expression of God's passion to communicate with us. It is 'alive and active' (Hebrews 4:12). To this very day, God still speaks through it to those who come to it with open hearts and minds. It is the principal means by which, now, 'God does speak' (Job 33:14).

There is one more thing Elihu wants to say to Job before he invites him to respond, and it again shows how carefully he has been listening to Job: he suggests how a mediator might help him.

> Yet if there is an angel at their side
>   a messenger, one out of a thousand,
>   sent to tell them how to be upright,
> and he is gracious to that person and says to God,
>   'Spare them from going down to the pit;
>   I have found a ransom for them –
> let their flesh is renewed like a child's'…
> That person can pray to God and find favour with him.
> JOB 33:23–26

There is something tentative about Elihu's proposal as if he was unsure whether he was offering too much, yet it is an offer which believers in a later age will discover to be wonderfully real. Here, surely, is a finger pointing towards Jesus, to the ministry he will one day fulfil for all who put their hope in him.

> For there is one God and one mediator between God and mankind, the man Christ Jesus, who gave himself as a ransom for all people.
> 1 TIMOTHY 2:5–6

He is able to save completely those who come to God through
him, because he always lives to intercede for them.
HEBREWS 7:25

There is hope, Job!

God does all these things to a person –
   twice, even three times –
to turn them back from the pit,
   that the light of life may shine on them.
JOB 33:29–30

As John said to encourage Christians facing persecution:

This is how we know that we belong to the truth and how we
set our hearts at rest in his presence: if our hearts condemn us,
we know that God is greater than our hearts.
1 JOHN 3:19–20

Far be it from God: chapters 34—35

Start here: read chapter 34
- Elihu addresses the three friends and restates Job's claim of innocence
- It is unthinkable that God is unjust
- God sees all that we do and think, so how is Job's claim to be explained?

Continue: read chapter 35
- Elihu now addresses Job
- Is God affected by our behaviour?

The consensus among commentators on these two chapters is that they are confusing! Elihu seems to contradict what he has said and will yet say. It is almost as if he loses his place in his notes and is reduced to saying the first thing that comes into his head while he tries to get back on track, as he will do shortly.

On the one hand, the three friends have made Job out to be in the wrong, while, on the other hand, Job has vehemently protested his innocence. In saying that Job is in the wrong, the friends have implied that God has been right to punish him, whereas Job accuses God of injustice – and that is his problem because he knows that God is just. In responding to this, Elihu explains that God is in a position to know whether or not Job has sinned. He sees the way men behave and takes note of what they do (34:21–25). Elihu then imagines that the friends have convinced someone of his sin, how should that person respond to God? He puts the question back to them for an answer.

> Suppose someone says to God,
>   'I am guilty but will offend no more…'
> Should God then reward you on your terms,
>   when you refuse to repent?
> You must decide, not I;
>   so tell me what you know.
> JOB 34:31–33

If Job 'speaks without knowledge', then tell him what to do! Elihu seems to be pressing the friends to see that the answer they have given is no answer at all.

In chapter 35, it is still more difficult to discern the thrust of the argument because it sounds as though Elihu has adopted the same position as Eliphaz and the others, and has abandoned his own. He seems to say that our sins, our prayers and indeed our very existence are a matter of complete indifference to God – which is obviously out of tune with what he has been saying so far. God, he seems to say, doesn't answer our prayers because he is not interested. Or is Elihu here describing what life is like for the person who has so resisted God's love that they have become incapable of responding to God – and he to them? People cry out in the midst of oppression, but not to God. They plead for help, but not from God. If they were to address God, there would be hope for them. God will give songs to those who turn to him, reasons for joy, in the darkest situations. Our Maker is near, one who knows and understands us better than anyone else. He is aware of our strengths and our weaknesses; he understands our vulnerabilities:

> But no one says, 'Where is God my Maker,
>   who gives songs in the night,
> who teaches us more than he teaches the beasts of the earth
>   and makes us wiser than the birds in the sky?'
> JOB 35:10–11

Again, Job makes no response.

There is more to be said: chapters 36—37

Bear with me a little longer and I will show you that there is more to be said on God's behalf.

JOB 36:2

Start here: read chapter 36
- God does not in fact ignore human beings
- God uses suffering purposefully and how we respond is critical
- A hymn to God's power in the world

Continue: read chapter 37
- The power of God in the snowstorm
- The power of God in the natural world
- Who are we to challenge him?

Does the opening verse of chapter 36 – 'Elihu continued' – suggest an awkward pause? There is the hint of an apology as he begins his fourth and final speech: 'Bear with me a little longer.'

Elihu recognises God's intense interest in the world and its inhabitants. He sees God's concern in the raindrops and the flood, in the streams and the oceans. And he is concerned for people too. Although Eliphaz, Bildad and Zophar had high views of God's greatness and glory, his holiness and justice, yet there is a hint of vindictiveness in their doctrine of God. They see him as bent on catching us out in our sin and taking pleasure in our punishment. Elihu too expects that God's right demands will be met, but he reflects something more.

> God is mighty, but despises no one…
>> He does not take his eyes off the righteous.
>
> JOB 36:5, 7

To those who say that a God of love would not punish us for our sin, the Bible responds that because God is love he must punish sin. His love led to the ultimate punishment of sin – in the death of Jesus. Yet one could not admire, let alone love, a god who wants only to punish, who has no wish to encourage or bless those who trust him. This has no echo in Elihu's theology.

> [God] tells them what they have done –
>> that they have sinned arrogantly.
> He makes them listen to correction
>> and commands them to repent of their evil.
>
> JOB 36:9–10

But he warns that those who 'do not listen… will perish' (36:12).

Elihu's theology is very practical. He has obviously thought deeply about the problem of suffering and has looked for an answer that recognises Job's integrity while at the same time acknowledges the justice and love of God. He takes us beyond the blame game – whether the blame is laid on Job, which was the case of the three friends, or on God, which was the case of Job. And Elihu's solution is simplicity itself: they had been looking in the wrong direction.

Suppose the explanation for Job's suffering lies not in his past but in his future. Elihu had hinted at such a possibility in his very first speech (33:29–30), and returns to the theme in his final speech.

> Those who suffer he delivers in their suffering;
>> he speaks to them in their affliction.
> He is wooing you from the jaws of distress
>> to a spacious place free from restriction.
>
> JOB 36:15–16

It seems only a passing thought, but what a thought! It is relatively easy to grasp the idea that God may send suffering because of past sins, but that he may send it for some purpose yet to be fulfilled is more challenging. However, can or do we fit that into our doctrine of a God of love? Perhaps we need to step back and reflect on this.

We don't find it hard to believe that God is purposeful; everything points to that. To imagine that God created the universe on a passing whim, that everything that happens is pointless and random, would undermine any possibility of finding meaning and purpose in life. All is chance and time. The Bible reveals a God who, from the outset, had certain objectives in mind for his creation. We see him ready to respond to the devastating result of Adam's sin with a solution hinted at in his judgement on the serpent (Genesis 3:15). As we read through the Old Testament, there are pointers towards the working out of a plan of salvation. In his letters to the churches, Paul often writes of our becoming Christians as the fulfilment of God's plan.

For reflection: suffering with purpose

The idea that there could be a purpose for the future in our experiences of the present is certainly one that stands scrutiny. But is it too big a step to go from that to see it as the reason for a person's suffering, even our own? Consider an incident during the ministry of Jesus (read the story in John 9). It concerns a man noticed by the disciples as they were walking one day. He was blind and that prompted a question which they put to Jesus:

> Rabbi, who sinned, this man or his parents, that he was born blind?
> JOHN 9:2

It is the old 'sowing and reaping' mentality, still to be found hundreds of years after the time of Job and his friends – and still to be found in our own day in modified form. The answer Jesus gave must, for them, have been jaw-dropping:

'Neither this man nor his parents sinned,' said Jesus, 'but this happened so that the works of God might be displayed in him.'
JOHN 9:3

Jesus then mixed a paste of spit and dust, smeared it on the man's eyes and sent him to wash his face in the nearby pool of Siloam. When the paste was washed off, the man was miraculously able to see. Wonderful! But the implications of what Jesus said are a little disturbing. Before there could be such an amazing demonstration of God's power, there had to be a blind man, preferably one who had been blind from birth so that the miracle could be the more remarkable. This means that some 20 or 30 years before, a young couple discovered that their newborn baby boy could not see. Imagine the disappointment, the sense of loss, the heartache they must have felt. And then the struggle, with neighbours muttering behind their hands that the parents must have sinned, the boy learning to walk with difficulty, the pain of rejection by his peers. Imagine the questions about old age and how they would cope with the needs of a disabled son and no one to help in their increasing frailty. For decades, this family wondered what they had done to deserve this – they kept looking back, little knowing that their son held a promise that would be realised only when Jesus crossed his path.

There are many other examples of this to be found in the Bible. Do you know the story of Joseph? He was the flash young son of Jacob, a true 'daddy's boy' who offended his older brothers to the point that they decided to get rid of him. Their plan went well in that Joseph found himself in exile in Egypt and then in prison. He had every reason to ask, 'What have I done to deserve this?' His punishment was out of all proportion to his offences, until God intervened and he was not only released from prison but also given a key role in government. It was to result in the most remarkable rescue of a nation from starvation, and at the same time Joseph's family as well.

When finally Joseph's story was told to his brothers, he explained it in these terms:

God sent me ahead of you… to save your lives by a great deliverance.
GENESIS 45:7

You intended to harm me, but God intended it for good to accomplish what is now being done.
GENESIS 50:20

Surely the supreme example of this principle is Jesus himself. When he came into the world, it was the expression of a centuries-long promise that God made through the prophets, which is why we read from their writings every Christmas. Throughout his life, too, there is this sense that a purpose is being worked out. This comes to its climax when 'the hour has come' and Jesus is betrayed to be executed as a criminal by death on a cross. His suffering could not possibly have been as a punishment for his sins. God had already publicly expressed his approval of his Son Jesus (Matthew 17:5)! As Peter explained to the crowds in his very first sermon, the death and resurrection of Jesus was just what God had intended to fulfil the promise made through the prophets (see Acts 2:17–36).

There is a long list of many others who had to suffer terribly because it was necessary to God's future promises. You will find it at the end of Hebrews 11, the chapter which explains what faith is and how it works in practice. It concludes with these words:

These were all commended for their faith, yet none of them received what had been promised, since God had planned something better for us so that only together with us would they be made perfect.
HEBREWS 11:39–40

A testimony

It was a sad time for Ann; she cradled her newborn daughter in her arms and wept because the child would never know her father. He had died just a few weeks after the wedding, fighting for his country in World War II. It was not rare for a baby to be conceived in the weeks prior to call-up, but for Ann it was to prove particularly painful as her little girl would not develop normally but would have a learning disability. Even from the child's infancy, her mother worried about what would happen when she was no longer able to care for her daughter. She prayed for a Christian place of care where her daughter would be loved in her dependent adulthood.

There were many others like her, Christian families with a son or daughter who, because of a learning disability, would need to be supported in a Christian environment beyond the lifetime of the parent. Wherever there was such a family, there were prayers for that need. And for a long time, there was no obvious answer.

Then, on the very day a young man was invited to become the pastor of a church in East London, his wife gave birth to a baby girl they named Rachel. But in a few weeks, a shadow fell across that joy as the couple learned that Rachel had Down's syndrome. Their pastor called and shared with them a promise from the Bible:

> The God of all comfort... comforts us in all our troubles, so that we can comfort those in any trouble with the comfort we ourselves receive from God.
> 2 CORINTHIANS 1:4

They were soon to learn that their path through parenthood would be different with the challenge of disappointments and discrimination, along with the fears, prejudice and misunderstandings of society. It never occurred to David and Madeleine to think of Rachel as some sort of punishment for sin. Although her presence in their lives was not without pain, she was their loved and lovely child. But they did not feel the concern for the long-term issues shared by many others they met in the subculture of learning disability of which they now found themselves a part. They were still young and old age was a long way off, but as they had increasing contact with other families hoping for Christian care, they began to enquire as to what was available. They found almost nothing at all in the UK so they too began to pray that someone would do something. To their surprise, it turned out that David and Madeleine were to be that 'someone'.

They founded a charity, known for many years as A Cause for Concern, later to be called Prospects. It grew steadily until, after some decades, it was supporting over 400 people with learning disabilities in different parts of the country. Alongside this, they also initiated a Bible teaching ministry to help churches engage with people with learning disabilities living in their own area. Thousands of people with learning disabilities found their place in the kingdom of God as a result.

As we look back – yes, I am that David and Madeleine is my wife – we do so with tears because our Rachel died a few years ago. We also look back with a sense of wonder that what prompted many to express sympathy who saw Rachel's condition as tragic was intended by God to bring security and salvation to so many. And to realise that we were part of God's answer to the prayers of Ann and many others like her!

Elihu was so right – God does work purposefully in and through situations which seem to us bewildering and perhaps deeply painful.

> The question 'Why?' is transformed into 'For what purpose?'
> David Atkinson[19]

This is all well and good, but it does not explain to us the reasons for Job's suffering! Here is another case of what is true not being the truth about this situation. Another reminder that, in God's dealings with his children, there is sometimes mystery beyond our ability to fathom it. We have looked back and now forwards, but there is another direction to which Elihu now points us, and that is up.

> God's voice thunders in marvellous ways;
>   he does great things beyond our understanding.
> JOB 37:5

As we step into chapter 37, we sense a change in tempo, perhaps for Elihu, Job and the rest, a literal change of atmosphere. There is the sound of thunder, the clouds begin to mass and swirl, the rain begins to fall. The poetry becomes more vivid as if trying to capture what is happening around them.

> He loads the clouds with moisture,
>   he scatters his lightning through them.
> At his direction they swirl around
>   over the face of the whole earth
>   to do whatever he commands them.
> JOB 37:11–12

We see the rain falling, 'a mighty downpour', the animals scurrying for shelter, the labourer abandoning his outdoor work and then, as suddenly as it began, it stops and the sun shines brightly from the skies swept clean by the wind (37:21). And, as Elihu and the others crouch beneath the awesome majesty of God in the storm, we are brought back to the heart of the issue, the key to understanding God's ways:

> Therefore men fear [God],
>   surely all the wise of heart fear him.
> JOB 37:24[20]

In the stillness after the storm, all are poised and ready for another voice to be heard.

For you to consider

- God is greater than we are – in one sense that is self-evident! Why do we find it difficult to accept in practice? Why do we assume that we know best?

- Would you have a problem accepting advice from a younger person? If so, why?

- Do you have an experience which was difficult at the time but afterwards you saw to be beneficial? Write a journal entry exploring the lessons you learned from it.

Part III

It's beyond me (chapters 38—42:6)

How remarkable that the experience of one man has fascinated people separated by centuries and millennia, in diverse cultures, living in vastly different settings. Even though there is so much we do not know about Job, we recognise the despair of pain, the grief and loss resulting from tragedy, natural disaster and human greed. If the book of Job had ended with the speeches of Elihu, we would still be attracted by this poignant poetry, but it would offer little by way of illumination on our own pathway or hope in our own sadnesses. Like Job, we would continue to ask the same unanswerable questions. But, thankfully, the book has not ended. The most important chapters are still to be explored.

8

Job has another visitor

My ears had heard of you
but now my eyes have seen you.
JOB 42:5

The storm that Elihu described passes through, the clouds part
and the sun comes out once more (37:22) – but not for long. Clouds
gather once more on the horizon, dark and threatening; the air
grows heavy, the breeze strengthens, the air chills and nature falls
silent. After days of discussion and debate, conversation on the
rubbish dump stalls. There is an expectant stillness as if there was
something other-worldly about a seemingly natural phenomenon.
And then, from the depths of eternity, with a commanding, awesome
gentleness, a voice that seems to penetrate to the very core of their
beings and makes the hair start up on the back of their necks:

Then the Lord spoke to Job out of the storm.
JOB 38:1

Elihu was right when he said: 'God does speak – now one way, now
another – though no one perceives it' (33:14).

But there will be no doubting that God is speaking this time. At last,
Job will have what he has demanded: 'Let the Almighty answer
me' (31:35). He had complained that God was elusive, that it was
impossible to confront him, hinting at the unfairness of his ways.

If I go to the east, he is not there;
if I go to the west, I do not find him.

> When he is at work in the north, I do not see him;
>> when he turns to the south, I catch no glimpse of him.
>
> JOB 3:8–9

But now the search is over; Job will have the opportunity he sought to put his case. God has found Job! The God of the universe has heard the cries of this sickly, ill-tempered man settled among the rotting garbage of an out-of-the-way community and has come to him where he is in response to his cries. What grace is this! And this is the Old Testament, remember, where the popular misconception is that God is the harsh judge of human weakness. Here is a glimpse before its time of the 'kindness and love of God' of which Paul wrote centuries later (Titus 3:4).

God's coming in the clouds and storm might suggest that Job had been right to think that God had abandoned him and put himself out of reach, but was now returning. It quickly becomes apparent in what God says to Job, and later to his friends, that in fact he had been present all along. He had heard Job's anger and argument and the rationalising of his friends. God had been at the dump then as much as he was in the storm now. Don't skip this fact as if it were incidental, an unimportant detail. God has committed himself to being with those who trust in him. He did so to the Israelites through Moses (Deuteronomy 31:8), to Joshua as he took up the leadership of God's people (Joshua 1:5), through the psalmist (94:14), and Isaiah (42:16). Jesus, also known as Emmanuel (which means 'God with us'), made this same promise to his followers:

> I will not leave you as orphans; I will come to you.
>
> JOHN 14:18

> Surely I am with you always, to the very end of the age.
>
> MATTHEW 28:20

And, lest there should be any doubt, God has said:

Never will I leave you; never will I forsake you.
HEBREWS 13:5

Theologians speak of the omnipresence of God, as always and everywhere present. Not 'in', as the pantheists teach, but 'with': personally alongside of each one, whether or not we sense or feel that divine proximity. This is a precious truth to hold close to our hearts when our circumstances seem to suggest that we are alone, abandoned even by God. It simply cannot be the case and, though faith may struggle to respond, we must learn to put our hand through the surrounding mists and touch the presence of God.

The name of God

Up to this point in the book of Job, God has been referred to respectfully and reverently by his name El Shaddai, God Almighty. God's arrival on the scene is announced using another of his names, Yahweh. This is the God of covenant, the God in relationship with those who trust him. In the New Testament, it morphs into 'Abba, Father'. As disaster had crushed Job, as his health collapsed, as his heart was torn with grief, God had seemed the more distant. But by restoring this name as he comes to Job, Yahweh reminds Job that there is a covenant between them where his 'presence' is not merely about proximity but about relationship. For God to abandon his child is utterly inconceivable, for it would be to break his own word; it would contradict his very name. No matter the message of our emotions, for those who know God at all he is always our Father.

Where can I go from your Spirit?
    Where can I flee from your presence?
If I go up to the heavens, you are there;
    if I make my bed in the depths, you are there.
If I rise on the wings of the dawn,
    if I settle on the far side of the sea,

> even there your hand will guide me,
>   your right hand will hold me fast.
>
> PSALM 139:7–10

God's tone of voice

The most direct and the most effective way to communicate with another person is face-to-face. Words can flow easily, given added meaning by the tone of voice and framed by body language. To shout or whisper, gesture with a frown and clenched fist or a smile and an open palm – these will all affect the way our speech is heard and our meaning is understood. A writer has a more laborious task in that he or she must set one letter after another to form words, then word after word to create sentences. The reader then reverses the process, recognising words from letter sequences and sentences from strings of words. Gradually, the message emerges from the text. But how should someone understand what they read? What emotion was the writer feeling as they wrote? What mood do they want to convey? Will the spirit of the message be understood by the reader? How can the right response be assured? It is a dilemma every letter or email writer knows all too well! How many misunderstandings there must be because of misread messages.

In the whole of the book of Job, the following chapters are by far the most instructive and important. If we are to understand the book at all, we must properly interpret the divine intervention they record. But with what tone of voice shall we hear what God has to say? Does he speak in anger or with irony? Are these questions real or rhetorical? Is this rebuke or repartee?

When we look at the text itself, it offers little help. We need to step back a little to consider what God says in a wider context. Nothing in the rest of the book of Job suggests that God is angry with Job. We saw this in the Prologue (1:8; 2:3), and we will see it again shortly in the Epilogue (42:7). This immediately softens God's questioning from that of an irritated superior reprimanding a subordinate to something more enquiring, more teasing even. Everything we read of God's attitude to his servant suggests that God loves Job deeply.

If we step back further and view the exchange in the light of biblical teaching at large, the probability that God is as wrathful as the questioning might suggest diminishes still more. The notion that God would crush the broken and battered Job just does not fit with what the rest of scripture teaches.

> The whole outlook of mankind might be changed if we could all believe that we dwell under a friendly sky and that the God of heaven, though exalted in power and majesty, is eager to be friends with us.
> A.W. Tozer[21]

God answers Job

The loss Job felt most keenly was not the loss of his business, his wealth, his reputation or even of his ten children: it was the companionship of God. The apparent absence of God was the deepest loneliness for Job.

> If only I knew where to find him;
>   if only I could go to his dwelling!
> JOB 23:3

Now God has come, though he had never gone away, and he invites Job, as it were, to join him on a tour of the universe. Job's attention is redirected away from his dreadful sores and the now-familiar and depressing piles of rubbish among which he sits. As a grandparent might take the hand of a petulant grandchild and lead them into the garden pointing out this lovely flower, that oddly shaped stone, the shadows rippling on the grass, until the child is once more peaceable, so now God turns Job's anger to wonder.

Job obviously needed a lesson in natural history, to be reminded of what he knew and didn't know. The tour takes in cosmology and meteorology and zoology and more! Job needed to be taken out of his preoccupation with himself and his pain, with his obsession with explaining the inexplicable, and, yes, from the terrible isolation of not being understood by those closest to him. Though he was already out of doors, he needed to see the outdoors as he had never seen it before in order to learn something about God that would transform his present and his future.

Christians have tended to caution about natural religion and its place in God's purposes. The assault on scripture from the bastions of atheism, apparently wielding the power of science with its mantra 'the survival of the fittest', intimidates journalists, policymakers and researchers to the extent that few – even Christians – feel confident to challenge science, despite its deficiencies.

Those who obstinately still believe that God alone can create something from nothing can accept without difficulty what science can demonstrate – as distinct from its speculative theories. They also accept that the fittest survive; it is obvious to every observer of the natural world, be they horticulturist or gardener, professor of agriculture or farmer, ornithologist or little child watching the blackbird nest in the front hedge. Of course, the strongest plants, pigs and pigeons are most likely to survive! And we also have no problem admitting that natural selection takes place as a result. We need to regain confidence in a biblical perspective on the universe we occupy. This is not the place to develop the argument. Others have done so fully and with greater skill than I can muster.[22]

Let us recognise the importance of seeing our place in God's wonderful world and be excited by it. Let us recapture our sense of wonder at this amazing place in which we live with other amazing creatures, large and small, surrounded by amazing plants that feed our need for nourishment and beauty, under amazing skies, where diversity and magnificence are such that all our superlatives are inadequate to describe what we see. It is simply wonder-full! To feel the sun on our faces, the wind in our hair, the grass beneath our feet, the soil between our fingers, the rain on our cheeks, this should be our welcome enjoyment of God's gift to us. And when you tire of the familiar, if ever, then take yourself on a clear night to a place beyond the streetlights and the traffic to look up into the Milky Way, to see the stars and planets and meteors in a vast array. Imagine God's challenge to Abraham: count the stars, and wonder!

There are lessons we too should learn when we go outside; it is there to teach us. We will see ourselves in a new light.

> When I consider your heavens,
>   the work of your fingers,
> the moon and the stars,
>   which you have set in place,
> what is mankind that you are mindful of them,
>   human beings that you care for them?
> You have made them a little lower than the angels
>   and crowned them with glory and honour.
> PSALM 8:3–5

And we will discover vital truth about God.

> What may be known of God is plain to them, because God has made it plain to them. For since the creation of the world God's invisible qualities – his eternal power and divine nature – have been clearly seen, being understood from what has been made.
> ROMANS 1:19–20

Job, perhaps like us, needed a refresher course! So what may we learn of God as we listen in to God's instruction?

The evidence of God's wisdom: chapters 38—39

Start here: read chapters 38 and 39
- God speaks out of the storm about the created world and the heavens
- God speaks about the animal kingdom

The poetry is dazzling, the illustrations vivid, the lesson profound, and it is seen as we look at the familiar from a fresh perspective. Have you ever wondered, Job, about the foundations of the world? As you built new sheds to shelter your camels and flocks from storms and houses for your family, and knew they must have good foundations, did you never ask how the earth itself on which you built was so stable? As you laid out your plans, did you never wonder how the dimensions of the earth were determined and measured? As you heard your builders urging one another on with songs, did you never wonder whether the stars sang as the earth took shape? How wise must he be who imagined and created with such a concern for stability and beauty?

Or the sea, Job, when you have travelled a long way from home and seen the waves beating on the shore, have you ever wondered why there are beaches at all (38:8)? As you saw its waves roll in, did you ever wonder what marvels might lie beneath them in the unseen depths (38:16)? What does Job know of the realm of death, of the source of light and darkness, of the storage system for snow and hail and rain, of lightning and the east wind?

With question after question, one word picture tumbling into another, God challenges the limits of Job's knowledge to bring home to him that there is a wisdom so great as to be beyond even the questions Job can ask, let alone the answers he might struggle to give. Gently, firmly and repeatedly, God presses the point home: tell me if you understand, tell me if you know all this, surely you know! Who? Who? Who? God asks. Have you? Have you? Have you? he persists. Can you? Do you? Can you? Do you? – the evidence mounts that Job is at the limit of his powers: far, far beneath what is required to understand, let alone create and sustain, what God shows him.

Attention shifts from storms and stars to birds and beasts. Have you ever wondered, Job, how the vast variety of creatures live and are sustained? From lions to donkeys, ravens to eagles, mountain goats to wild oxen, from the laughter of horses and the silliness of the ostrich, God ranges over the incredible diversity of the creatures that share our planet. Who feeds them? How are their populations kept in balance? Even though he is a farmer, Job's wisdom falls far short of offering any answers. And when God adds to the list one animal that has been domesticated – the horse – he speaks of it, in breathtaking poetry, in terms of the battlefield rather than the field where crops are grown. So, again, Job must acknowledge God's higher wisdom.

What is striking about these chapters is how unscientific they are! The sceptic would pour scorn on the idea that snow and hail is kept in some celestial cupboard, mocking the ignorance of primitive religion – and, in the process, show how completely they have missed the point. God is not challenging Job's knowledge, or ours; the challenge is to his wisdom, his understanding. Science has certainly provided us with a vast array of data and information about the world. It is factual, clinical and useful, but it does not, cannot, tell us why these things are, or why they are as they are, or even why they exist at all, why there is something rather than nothing. It offers us no poetry with which to praise, no mystery to make us marvel, no wonder to make us wise. For that, we need to look beyond the data to the Designer, beyond the matter to the Maker, beyond the scientist to God himself.

In all his struggles with the mystery of suffering, Job needed to see again that God is wise beyond our highest and most profound concept of wisdom. Every question science answers provokes further questions, because there is more to be known than we can ever compute. In the same way, at every point at which we think we have understood God's ways, another window opens and we see whole worlds of possibility yet to be appreciated.

And still the storm swirls around Job, its very power reinforcing God's gentle but persistent challenge.

> Will the one who contends with the Almighty correct him?
>   Let him who accuses God answer him!
> JOB 40:2

The evidence of God's power: chapters 40—41

Start here: read chapters 40 to 42:6
- God's challenge and Job's response
- The implications of Job's charge and his response
- The power of the behemoth
- The power of the leviathan
- Job's repentance

Job has made some serious allegations against God and these are addressed seriously by God. Job has justified himself as being in the right and has implied that God is in the wrong to the point that, in God's opinion, Job has discredited God's justice. To do that, Job, you need to be something you are not, God says.

> Do you have an arm like God's,
>   and can your voice thunder like his?
> Then adorn yourself with glory and splendour,
>   and clothe yourself in honour and majesty.
> JOB 40:9–10

And, once you have demonstrated your power over the proud and powerful, you won't need me, God seems to say.

> Then I myself will admit to you
>   that your own right hand can save you.
> JOB 40:14

Job is a very long way from possessing such power, let alone exercising it, as God proceeds to demonstrate. God brings into focus two animals described in all the untamed wildness of their powers: the behemoth and the leviathan. What are these fearsome beasts? Some commentators speculate that they are monsters, creatures of myth drawn from the imagery and legends of Job's times. It hardly seems likely that God would resort to fables when clearly his goal is to teach Job truth about himself.

There is general agreement that the behemoth is what we know as the hippopotamus and the leviathan is the crocodile. The descriptions are immediately recognisable – the thighs of the hippo being like bronze tubes, the scales of the crocodile like armour. These are creatures of immense strength, seemingly invulnerable to the power of human beings, beyond the force of pre-ballistic weapons, able to withstand raging torrents. Imagine trying to put a bridle on a crocodile, God teases, so that you could take it home as a pet for your girls (41:5). Yet even these wildest of wild ones belong to God and are under his control.

> Everything under heaven belongs to me.
> JOB 41:11

This is important truth for Job to rediscover – and for us too. Without doubt, he believed in the sovereignty of God: his name for God had been El Shaddai, God Almighty. Of course, he understood that God is the creator of the world. But he must realise that this is not dogma for theologians but truth for every day, for every believer – for us too. This is deeply practical theology on which both the hippopotamus and the crocodile depend – and so do we. Paul focuses this truth in Jesus:

> For in him all things were created: things in heaven and on earth, visible and invisible, whether thrones or powers or rulers or authorities; all things have been created through him and for him. He is before all things, and in him all things hold together.
> COLOSSIANS 1:16–17

Job's response:
chapters 40:3–5; 42:1–6

Job was given two opportunities to respond. God, as it were, calls him to the bar to present his case. Let him who accuses God answer him (40:2). This is exactly what Job had demanded (23:4–5; 31:35). Imagine the privilege. What will he say? He has had so much time to decide his arguments, has in part rehearsed them before his friends. Surely Job will ask again the question with which he has greeted every sunrise and sunset since that day when his life was so devastated. This is Job's big moment! Listen carefully to what he says:

> I am unworthy – how can I reply to you?
>   I put my hand over my mouth.
> I spoke once, but I have no answer –
>   twice, but I will say no more.
> JOB 40:4–5

But Job, God hasn't answered you! Admittedly he has spoken, but in all that cascade of questions he has not given even a hint of an explanation for your sufferings, nor has he denied his part in them. Has God missed the point?

Perhaps there are more important questions than this. If God had given Job an explanation of what had been happening, would Job have understood? If Job knew what we, the readers, know, would that have helped him cope with the bewilderment he felt? The challenge of Satan and God's response would have to be explained and why God chose Job for the testing. The theology might be tricky for him but the sense of unfairness would be greater. The questions would remain.

When a little child asks us to explain something too complex for their years, we promise to tell them when they are older, when their understanding of the world around them can bear the greater knowledge. So it is for us in respect of some spiritual realities; we do not have an adequate frame of reference within which to understand some issues which are the purview of eternity and deity. We are too limited, our wisdom is too finite and we have to trust our Father.

Job stands, or kneels, head bowed. 'I am unworthy!' is his best response. He has been humbled, yes, but not humiliated. Now he sees, as never before, how limited has been his understanding, his wisdom. He is embarrassed to realise how much he has dared to say. 'I will say no more' (40:3).

After God has finished speaking, Job does so once more.

> You [God] asked, 'Who is this that obscures my plans without knowledge?'
>   Surely I spoke of things I did not understand,
>   things too wonderful for me to know.
> JOB 42:3

Has Job reached his lowest point, crushed by the weight of God's hand bearing down on his pain-soaked suffering? Not at all. He has seen things he had never seen before and in God's company had begun to understand, if not the extent of God's wisdom, at least the limits of his own. And yet in that encounter, he had learned more of God than he thought possible: 'things too wonderful for me to know'. Of course, he regretted much of what he had said. Of course, he felt ashamed that he had doubted the power and goodness of God. It is right that he should repent of this, but his eyes are filled with wonder not tears, with joy not shame.

> My ears had heard of you
>   but now my eyes have seen you.
> JOB 42:5

How do you react to God's intervention? Do you find it frustrating or encouraging? God's route for us through our suffering is completely different from that which we might have chosen. Along the way, there may be medication, pastoral care, therapy, counselling, even direct and miraculous healing – any one of the many options helpfully on offer in the 21st century. Hopefully, by whatever means, we will find help to progress through pain or grief or anguish. God has his own pathway for us which goes beyond the physical, the psychological and the emotional to touch the very core of who and what we are. That pathway may even be to open our eyes to the world around us through which he will speak as his Spirit meets us to bring us hope.

For Job, to find peace he had to see the wisdom and power of God. The way through his pain was the fear of the Lord, for he was never more in awe of God than after this encounter. Most of his questions remain unanswered as no new information, no clear explanation was given. But never was Job wiser than after seeing glimpses of a wisdom and power infinitely beyond his comprehension, and by that route he found the grace to trust his covenant-keeping God.

For you to consider

- There is a world of difference between information and experience. How is Job's discovery reflected in your experience?

- Do you have unanswered questions about your or someone else's suffering? How would it help if you went out and learned from the world around you more about the wisdom and power of God?

- Job read the only 'book' of revelation God had given him – the natural world. Having helped another person to see God there, where in scripture would you take them to see the lines more clearly drawn of God's grace to those who trust him?

- If there are 'things too wonderful for [us] to know' (42:3), what difference will this make to the way you cope with suffering?

9

Epilogue

The Lord blessed the latter part of Job's life more than the former part.

JOB 42:12

Start here: read chapter 42:7–17
- God rebukes and instructs Job's friends
- God restores Job to his family
- God blesses Job with renewed prosperity

We have reached the climax – or, some would say, the anticlimax – of the book of Job. Like an Agatha Christie plot, suddenly everything seems to fall into place as we race towards the story's end. Some regard it as too much like a fairy story where the hero and his bride 'live happily ever after': too much sweetener for some tastes. But perhaps things are not quite as they appear on first reading.

With the change from poetry to prose, there is a change of mood and pace. We might have thought that with Job's repentance the storm would pass and the voice of God fall silent. The three friends might prepare to go home at last, feeling that their job was well done, their journey worthwhile. Not so! We feel the pulse of real life here, not fiction or fantasy. There is another reckoning still to take place.

From the swirling storm clouds, God speaks again, but this time to Eliphaz as the representative of the three friends. And it is not praise we hear. We can only assume that they may have listened to the exchanges between God and Job, or at least to Job's side of the conversation. It seems unlikely that they had been party to the mind-stretching vision of the universe that God shared with Job. What God has to say to Eliphaz must have come as a shock to him. Given that the friends had taken so much time to support Job, had put up with dreadful conditions day after day on the filthy tip, under the burning sun, in order to share their insights out of a genuine desire to help him find a way through his pain, they might have expected some commendation from God. But it is not praise they receive; in fact, God is not in the least approving of their efforts.

> I am angry with you and your two friends, because you have not spoken the truth about me, as my servant Job has.
> JOB 42:7

God repeats his criticism, reinforcing how serious it is in his view. We may feel that this is rather harsh on God's part, especially since God seemed to treat Job's accusations of him lightly. There were, however, significant differences between the implications of what the friends said and Job's remarks.

God says of Job's friends: 'You have not spoken the truth about me.' They were seen to have misrepresented God. Since most of what they had said was directed at and critical of Job, this seems a little strange. However, as we saw earlier, their core argument was that Job's sufferings were punishment for his sins, which could be alleviated if Job would admit his wrongs and repent. They had no evidence of wrongdoing on Job's part; indeed, all the evidence they had and all that they knew of their friend was that he was a good man. They had arrived at their mistaken conviction by inverting a biblical principle. 'What you sow you reap' had been turned on its head to mean that 'what you reap you must have sown'! It was false theology and completely unjust at the same time. It implicated God by suggesting Job's suffering was divine punishment for sin when no sin had been committed. That would make God responsible for gross injustice! The three friends were the wise men of their day, the counsellors and teachers to whom others would turn for help and advice. They should have known better and were answerable for such serious error.

God's rebuke of Eliphaz and his friends needs to be carefully considered. In our enthusiasm to be helpful, we may be wrong to the point that we actually misrepresent God. That is a solemn charge. James warns us that teachers face stricter judgement (James 3:1). The potential harm they may do is incalculable since it may have eternal consequences for them as well as the person they are keen to help.

Even as God rebukes, he shows mercy, holding out to the friends the offer of a way back, of a means of forgiveness. It involves sacrifice! Somehow, even the word itself repels us; it seems so very Old Testament: slaughter, blood, fire, altars! In fact, it is very 'Bible', for it is found throughout and takes us to the heart of the meaning of forgiveness and its cost.

From beginning to end, the Bible takes sin extremely seriously. What we might excuse as a minor misdemeanour, the Bible regards as something deeply offensive to God. The punishment of sin, its 'price' you might say, is death, which is separation from God. It was the arrangement made in the garden of Eden between God and Adam (Genesis 2:17) and first experienced by Adam and his wife Eve when they were excluded from the garden following the first sin (Genesis 3:24). As Paul puts it long after: 'The wages of sin is death' (Romans 6:23).

It is this connection with death that gives the sacrificial system its compelling logic: 'Without the shedding of blood there is no forgiveness' (Hebrews 9:22). The death of the sacrificial lamb substitutes for the death of the person who sinned, which is why John the Baptist spoke of Jesus as 'the Lamb of God'. The death of Jesus was our death, the punishment he suffered our punishment, so that the forgiveness we need can be granted to all those who put their faith in him.

Eliphaz was assured that his sin and that of Bildad and Zophar could be forgiven if they offered sacrifices. It was the only option they were offered; it is the only option possible. Contrary to popular religion, we cannot hope for forgiveness simply by trying harder and doing better. Nothing is resolved by this. The three friends would surely have preferred some other way, as the route God offered required them to face up to their own mistakes. Job was vindicated: he was right; they were wrong. They would have to ask Job to be their priest and act on their behalf.

The times we live in are very different from those in which this scene was first played out, but the fundamentals of our relationship with God are little changed. We, like Eliphaz and friends, need to be forgiven and we must walk the same path of sacrifice, though in our case it has already been made:

> He [Jesus] himself bore our sins in his body on the cross.
> 1 PETER 2:24

What a reversal of roles for Eliphaz, Bildad and Zophar – but they accepted it. So too did Job, acting to bless the very people who had misunderstood him and accused him of terrible wrongs. Now he must act as their mediator and intercessor. The friends must go to find and buy the animals while Job turns the tip into a temple, building an altar and lighting a fire. The offerings are made and accepted. Forgiveness flows.

Perhaps it is at this point that the storm passes and once again the sun shines over the friends, now joined even more deeply by their shared experiences of God – his rebuke and his mercy. What next? We are not told in any detail, but we may note that it was only after Job had prayed and the Lord had accepted his prayer that his circumstances began to change: 'the Lord restored his fortunes' (42:10). Soon his family and friends want to see him again, so presumably the healing process is well under way and he is able to receive them and their consolation and their gifts. His marriage must be rebuilt from the near disaster of grief and bitterness of earlier days, restoring trust and lost intimacy once more. Over time, the home will once again ring with the cries and laughter of children. Building a family is a process of years, not moments. Similarly, rebuilding his business must take time: restoring his run-down estate, replanting his fields, buying and breeding animals to restock the sheds and stalls empty for so long. Staff must be hired and re-hired into an effective team to share the load as once more God blesses the integrity with which Job conducts his affairs. As the story is told, it seems to take but a moment, but the process must have stretched out over years.

For Job, the blessing of renewed prosperity must have been tinged with sadness. There were ten graves to be tended, memories to be revisited of happy days with those now taken from him. There were widows to be cared for, the families of previous staff killed while about Job's business in those earlier tragedies. Grief may soften with time but never ends. Perhaps in his own body too, there were scars and even ongoing weaknesses from the devastating illness which had invaded his flesh. But all of these things could not take away from the most precious aspect of his recovery: the restored companionship of God. What he had seen that day on the rubbish heap, what he had heard and learned of Yahweh, his covenant God, remained with him to the end when, 140 years later, he died 'an old man and full of years' (42:17).

Looking back to go forward

We know that in all things God works for the good of those who love him… What, then, shall we say in response to these things? If God is for us, who can be against us? He who did not spare his own Son, but gave him up for us all – how will he not also, along with him, graciously give us all things?
ROMANS 8:28, 31–32

It is time to reflect on some of the lessons learned, to return to some of the themes we have touched on during our journey through the book of Job and wonder where they fit in the context in which we must live our own life of faith. There are some difficult issues to face, a way of thinking about God that may shake the very foundations of our understanding. There are things to be said that are not easy to say and may not be easy to hear.

Popular religion has shaped its god into someone who is warm and comfortable, who is kind and gentle, who can be relied upon to be nice to us. This is the deity that New Atheism mocks and rejects. How can such a god exist who allows so much suffering in the world he claims to have made? It is a fair jibe! It is belief in such a God that prompts our complaint that it is unfair when life serves up suffering and war and disease and death.

If Job's struggle teaches us anything, it teaches us that God is not 'nice'. There is a bigness about God that dwarfs us – dwarfs our virtue, our understanding, our theology. We do not have enough words in our vocabulary to describe him. His holiness is beyond our purest thoughts, his knowledge more comprehensive than the most encyclopaedic libraries can embrace, his wisdom beyond what the most profound philosophy can begin to deduce, his eternity simply unimaginable to time-bound thought.

How then are we to understand ourselves, our circumstances, our times? We want to understand; we need to understand, for we are creatures hardwired to expect life to have meaning. We live in a rational universe that functions according to largely predictable forces and patterns. But when life takes a turn we do not expect, we want to know why. We too would like to be able to scale down the immensity of God in order to put our questions and find out what is going on and why. Not surprisingly, many who turn to the book of Job do so hoping to find an answer to the problem of suffering. Surely here, in the story of one man's legendary experience of unrelenting pain, we can find a way of responding to that lifelong question: Why? So what can we say with certainty?

First, there are no easy answers! For Job's friends, there was one obvious explanation which, had Job been more honest with himself (in their view), he would have accepted. They were wrong. The reason for Job's suffering remained out of reach to them and to Job. They would never have come close to finding it even if they had debated for years.

Second, suffering cannot be explained as simply as drawing a straight line between sin and punishment. Granted, the Bible does make that link from time to time, both generally and in specific instances. Clearly the world would be a different place if sin had not entered. We see that in the consequences of Adam and Eve's sin (Genesis 3:14–19), and in the enormous contrast with the new heaven and earth (Revelation 21:1–8). God warned his people that disobedience would have physical and natural consequences such as famine and exile (e.g. Deuteronomy 28). Paul mentions that some Christians in Corinth were ill because they had abused the Lord's Supper (1 Corinthians 11:30), and James hints at the possibility of a link between sin and sickness in some cases (James 5:15). But to argue, as Job's friends did, that sickness is invariably punishment for sin is a serious mistake.

Third, Satan – or 'the Satan' as the book of Job describes the devil, intending to focus attention on his role as an adversary rather than his personhood – is limited in his power. He may accuse but is not at liberty to harm God's children except the Father permits it. We do not need to fear him if we remain close to God. In his classic tale, *Pilgrim's Progress*, John Bunyan imagines the devil as a lion on Christian's path, but he is chained! At the same time, we would be foolish to dismiss him as a figure of fun dressed in a red leotard carrying a three-pronged fork.

Fourth, if the book of Job has anything to teach us about suffering, it is not so much an explanation we need, but an experience of God himself, to learn the fear of God that gives wisdom. Disturbing that may be, but nothing will be more fulfilling, more likely to bring us peace. This was certainly the case for Job and can be for us, which is why, early on, I suggested that the book of Job is more about God than the human experience of tragedy and pain. What we learn from God here may seriously challenge what we have always believed about him. So, let's try to draw the threads together finally.

When Job stood among the ruins of his family and his business and felt disease spreading across his body, he reached out to comfort his distraught wife as he prepared to become an exile from her and the community. Gently, he posed the question that rings in our ears as we read page after page of poetic discussion:

> Shall we accept good from God, and not trouble?
> JOB 2:10

It is not so much a question as an affirmation, for the answer implied must be, 'Yes, of course we will!' But is it something we too can affirm – you and I? That is the question that remains for us to answer.

If we also say 'Yes', we thereby affirm our willingness to accept whatever God sends into our lives. That is an enormous step of trust in his loving purpose for us and those dear to us, for it is possible that God will take us along a path not unlike that which Job had to walk. We had better understand the implications.

God's purpose for his world is comprehensive and immense beyond our capacity to understand. So that Job could grasp this, God took him on a virtual tour of the universe. He brought into view its diversity and mystery, its tiny detail and its complexity. Job was shown constellations as well as the ostrich egg lying exposed on the desert floor. He was reminded of the strength of the crocodile as well as the shimmering beauty of its scales. With every fresh glimpse of the world around him, Job grew a little smaller and saw God as even greater. It would do us good to switch off our phones and tablets and TVs and step outside more often to experience the same change of perspective.

As we look into God's revelation of himself in the Bible, we learn that God is at work in the world fulfilling his purpose – and that purpose is all-encompassing. Paul begins his letter to Christians in Ephesus with a discussion of predestination – what a way to start a letter! If we leap over the verses argued about for centuries, we get to the heart of his amazing insight:

> [God] works out everything in conformity with the purpose of his will.
> EPHESIANS 1:11

Note this: God's purpose embraces 'everything' and he ensures that it does what he wants! What God determines, God does. We could start up the age-old debate about God's sovereignty and human responsibility, but it is unlikely that we will ever explain the relationship between the two. We end up giving greater importance to one or the other for different reasons. The fact is that this is a mystery and, if God had actually given a clear explanation, we would still be no wiser because it lies outside categories with which we are familiar. We are too finite, too limited to understand the 'everything', let alone how it can be made to function 'in conformity with the purpose of his will'.

To help us grasp the vastness of what Paul tells us here, let me offer an illustration. First, change 'everything' into 'everyone'. In the early years of Prospects, the charity my wife and I founded, I would interview potential staff. I remember meeting Julie to discuss a vacancy in a home for people with learning disabilities in Wales. She was qualified for the post, obviously capable, and she was single and able to move to the area of the home. Later, there was another vacancy in the home and David was appointed, again suited to the role for which he had applied, and single and therefore able to move to where he would work. In both cases, they and we felt sure that this was God's purpose. Some time later – you know what's coming – these two fell in love and married; they were convinced that God had brought them together. In due course, they had children. They moved on to other work and we lost touch but probably by now they are grandparents and in due course maybe they will be great-grandparents. Who knows how far they are spread out across the land? There were many other examples like this during the history of Prospects, perhaps scores of new families. So far as Madeleine and I were concerned, that was not part of our purpose, but clearly it was part of God's. And as a result, there could well be thousands of children in the United Kingdom and perhaps in other countries too, who can trace their heritage back to couples whom God brought together through the charity, all from one small beginning. If I struggle to understand God's purpose for so many interconnected lives across half a century, across towns and countries, it is little wonder that I cannot begin to grasp how God's 'everything' works towards his purpose. Is your God too small for that?

Job, however, takes us even deeper into this unfamiliar territory. His experiences require us to wonder whether God's 'everything' includes suffering. Is it really possible that God is mysteriously building into our lives situations which he knows will cause us pain, and doing so because that is part of his purpose? Surely not! A group of us were talking about this one Sunday evening because, as Christians, we wanted to understand what the Bible says about suffering. 'I'm a mother,' said one person, 'and I will do anything in my power to ensure that my children don't suffer. If I do that for my children, I believe my heavenly Father will do that for his children.' It was a powerful and moving argument, but is it right? It neatly absolves God from having to take any blame, but is it right? When we talk like this, are we not making God in our own image? If it is right, then Job is wrong to imply that we should accept trouble from God. God will send only what is good and will surely and powerfully keep his children from harm and danger. Trouble must therefore come from somewhere else, where God is not in control!

There are some very disturbing examples in the Bible of people whose suffering was obviously part of God's 'everything' purpose. Elijah was forced to take up temporary exile and be dependent on a widow for his keep. Jeremiah had to watch old friends being taken into exile and foreign armies taking control of his beloved Jerusalem. For Daniel, God's purpose took him into a den of lions and his three friends into a fiery furnace, showing their persecutors who was truly God. For Hosea, God's will required him to marry an ex-prostitute who didn't remain ex! For Ezekiel, the sudden death of his beloved wife was the worst of many awful sufferings God brought on him. For John the Baptist and James, one of the twelve disciples, God's 'everything' included martyrdom. The young church must have wondered if God was still in control, the more so when Peter was thrown into prison and Stephen was brutally murdered by the mob. But as you look back at the story of the church in the book of Acts, you see God's purpose being fulfilled as these seeming disasters force the church to take the message of the gospel deeper and deeper into the vast Roman Empire. Is your God too small to bear such heavy responsibility?

Day after day, the TV news forces us to confront what is happening in the world. We have to ask of this, too: are these things part of God's 'everything'? The wreckage of Syria, the tear-filled eyes of blank-faced children in the midst of war, the starving mothers holding to their dry breasts the limp bodies of babies too weak to suck, the broken homes and trees dashed by swirling floods and mudslides – how can these ever conform to the purpose of God's will? Of course, in many of these examples, the guilt lies heavily on the shoulders of hateful, greedy, thoughtless, selfish, violent human beings. But surely God does not stand by helplessly wringing his hands at wrongdoing, and if he doesn't, why does he allow such wickedness to seem to win?

I do not understand how God's will is worked out in one life in one place at one time; how can I possibly understand or explain the interconnectedness of God's power and mercy, purpose and grace at work across the world in the lives of billions of people? If God were to challenge me to attempt an explanation, I would have to say with Jeremiah, 'O Lord, you know' (Jeremiah 15:15, ESV). Job's suffering began with attacks by Sabeans and Chaldeans and also included natural disasters. He saw beyond the human agency: 'The hand of the Lord has done this' (Job 12:9). At no time did God contradict this!

Why does it surprise us when we experience difficulties? The Bible is clear in warning us that they will be part of our journey. James, the brother of Jesus, wants us to be not only accepting of the possibility but actually joyful in it!

> Consider it pure joy, my brothers and sisters, whenever you face trials of many kinds, because you know that the testing of your faith produces perseverance. Let perseverance finish its work so that you may be mature and complete, not lacking anything.
> JAMES 1:2–4

Paul offers similar encouragement:

> We also glory in our sufferings, because we know that suffering produces perseverance; perseverance, character; and character, hope. And hope does not put us to shame, because God's love has been poured out into our hearts through the Holy Spirit, who has been given us.
> ROMANS 5:3–5

Just hours before Jesus was arrested, he warned Peter of an impending personal crisis:

> Simon, Simon, Satan has asked to sift you as wheat. But I have prayed for you, Simon, that your faith may not fail.
> LUKE 22:31–32

Jesus had prayed for him, but still Simon Peter had to face the horror of Satan's assault and his own failure. Perhaps that painful period was in his mind when he wrote later:

> Dear friends, do not be surprised at the fiery ordeal that has come on you to test you, as though something strange were happening to you. But rejoice inasmuch as you participate in the sufferings of Christ.
> 1 PETER 4:12–13

Of course we will accept good from God – but trouble too?

> The book of Job has shown us that there are questions for which there are no answers this side of heaven, and problems human logic cannot solve. But it has also shown us the living God, a hidden God who makes his presence known sometimes through his apparent absence, a God whose encounter with us prevents us from tidying up every problem corner of our lives into neat manageable packages… There are some things which have, by their very nature, to be left within the mystery of God.[23]

Is that it, then? Do we just have to go for a walk and hope to drag a message of hope from the daisies and dandelions, wishing that God would show up and inspire in us the faith of Job? No, there is another way. God would take us to a different place, one that will revolt us far more than Job's rubbish heap. He will lead us up a hill on top of which, in ground soaked in blood, stand three rough wooden crosses. Freshly nailed to these crude timbers are two representatives of all our failing humanity, criminals convicted and punished for their crimes. And on the central cross, another person, three times declared innocent by Roman justice, twice approved by a voice from heaven itself, and yet condemned to die. And as the sky darkens at midday, this time by strange miracle rather than storm, the voice of God comes from the cross not the clouds, a cry of dereliction so awful as never to have been heard before or since:

> My God, my God, why have you forsaken me?
> MATTHEW 27:46

The earth itself trembles at the sound – and then finally a cry of triumph: 'Finished!' It is accomplished, as Jesus dismisses his spirit.

Was Pilate to blame? Yes, of course he was responsible. Had the Jewish crowd no guilt? Indeed, they had: 'His blood be on us,' they had cried. But it was my fault too, and yours:

> He himself bore our sins in his body on the cross.
> 1 PETER 2:24

Even in that awful death, it was God's purpose that was being fulfilled.

> Surely he took up our pain
>   and bore our suffering,
> yet we considered him punished by God,
>   stricken by him, and afflicted,
> But he was pierced for our transgressions,
>   he was crushed for our iniquities…
> Yet it was the Lord's will to crush him.
> ISAIAH 53:4–5, 10

This is the ultimate challenge of Job. Is our God too small for this? If we must live with knowing that the purpose of God includes 'everything', will we face the future – with all its potential for good and trouble, for joy and tears, for fulfilment and failure – with confidence in God's ability to achieve his goal and bring 'unity to all things… under Christ' (Ephesians 1:10), or are we left with an empty heaven, a meaningless world, an unresolvable 'problem of pain' and a too-small God?

> The fear of the Lord – that is wisdom.
> JOB 28:28

Notes

1 H.L. Ellison, *The International Bible Dictionary* (Tyndale House, 1980), p. 792.
2 R.H. Pfeiffer, *Introduction to the Old Testament*, p. 683 – quoted by Francis I. Andersen, *Job* (Inter-Varsity Press, 2008), p. 31.
3 Andersen, *Job*, p. 31.
4 Andersen, *Job*, p. 33.
5 Andersen, *Job*, p. 88.
6 From 'My God, I thank thee' by Adelaide A. Procter (1825–64).
7 David Atkinson, *The Message of Job* (Inter-Varsity Press, 1992), p. 36.
8 Atkinson, *The Message of Job*, p. 56.
9 Atkinson, *The Message of Job*, p. 57.
10 A.W. Tozer, *The Knowledge of the Holy* (James Clarke, 1965), p. 9.
11 Tozer, *The Knowledge of the Holy*, p. 7.
12 Atkinson, *The Message of Job*, p. 106.
13 Terry Eagleton, *The Meaning of Life* (Oxford University Press, 2007), p. 30.
14 Eagleton, *The Meaning of Life*, p. 80.
15 See Nabeel Qureshi, *Seeking Allah, Finding Jesus* (Zondervan, 2016), p. 105 onwards.
16 Andersen, *Job*, p. 238.
17 Atkinson, *The Message of Job*, p. 122.
18 C.S. Lewis, *The Problem of Pain* (Fontana, 1940), p. 81.
19 Atkinson, *The Message of Job*, p. 135.
20 As translated by Andersen, *Job*, p. 268.
21 Tozer, *The Knowledge of the Holy*, p. 89.
22 See the numerous books such as: Edgar Andrews, *Who Made God? Searching for a theory of everything* (EP Books, 2009); John C. Lennox, *God's Undertaker: Has science buried God?* (Lion, 2007); Alister McGrath, *The Great Mystery: Science, God and the human quest for meaning* (Hodder, 2017); and many others.
23 Atkinson, *The Message of Job*, p. 155.

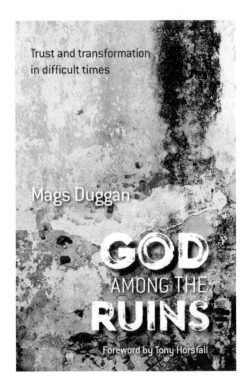

Trust and transformation
in difficult times

Mags Duggan

GOD
AMONG THE
RUINS

Foreword by Tony Horsfall

It takes courage to hope; to stand in our confusion and grief and still to believe that 'God is not helpless among the ruins'. Guided by Habakkuk and his prophetic landmarks, we are drawn on a reflective journey through the tangled landscape of bewildered faith, through places of wrestling and waiting, and on into the growth space of deepened trust and transformation. As you read, discover for yourself the value and practice of honest prayer, of surrender, of silence and listening, and of irrepressible hoping.

God among the Ruins
Trust and transformation in difficult times
Mags Duggan
978 0 85746 575 7 £7.99

brfonline.org.uk

Like the seasons themselves, our lives are variable and can change in a moment. In *Seasoned by Seasons*, Michael Mitton acknowledges this and offers Bible reflections for the variety of life's seasons: spring, the season of emerging new life; summer, the season of fruitfulness; autumn, the season of letting go; winter, the season of discovering light in the dark. What can we learn, and how can we be encouraged in each season of our lives? This book will empower you to discover for yourself the truths and messages of scripture, and might well transform the way you view life's changes.

Seasoned by Seasons
Flourishing in life's experiences
Michael Mitton
978 0 85746 540 5 £7.99

brfonline.org.uk

Bible readings for special times

Anxious Times

Carmel Thomason

Foreword by Archbishop John Sentamu

A book of 24 undated reflections drawing on a range of relevant Bible passages to offer genuine hope and encouragement in anxious times. Encompassing the very human emotions of fear and anxiety, the reflections encourage us to draw comfort and strength from God's word even in those times when he seems silent to us. This book acknowledges that trust and hope in God's goodness doesn't always come easily, but when embraced we gain the strength to face our fear with courage and confidence.

Anxious Times
Bible readings for special times
Carmel Thomason
978 0 85746 660 0 £3.99

brfonline.org.uk